LETTERS PATENT

A PRACTICAL
THEOLOGY OF WORK

Graham Leo

a. Acorn Press

Published by Acorn Press
An imprint of Bible Society AustraliaACN 148 058 306
Charity licence 19 000 528
GPO Box 4161
Sydney NSW 2001
Australia
www.acornpress.net.au | www.biblesociety.org.au

ISBN 978-0-647-53044-3

First published by Morning Star Publishing in 2020,
ISBN 978-0-647-53049-8

NATIONAL LIBRARY OF AUSTRALIA

A catalogue record for this work is available from the National Library of Australia

Design and typesetting: John Healy

DEDICATION

To Diane, Kay and Nina, and especially Elaine.

These generous women have worked with me as my personal assistants in my role as principal in two schools over 25 years. They have borne my burdens with me; they have prayed for me; they have laughed and cried with me; and they have helped me when I most needed help.

Elaine, I know, still prays for me daily, even though I have been retired for over five years from the role where we worked together. Her prayers for me and for my wife, Mieke, have sustained me more than any of us could possibly have imagined.

During the delay between submission to publisher and final editing, my beautiful wife passed away after a long battle with cancer. She so wanted this book to see the light of day before she went, but sadly, it was not to be. Thank you, Mieke, for your constant love and support.

ACKNOWLEDGEMENTS

I want to acknowledge the care and attention to detail that was given to me by my two supervisors in my Doctor of Ministry Research Project. That project formed the basis of this book.

Reverend Doctor Gordon Preece and Doctor Neil Holm provided me with careful and frequent advice as I was doing my research and writing up my final thesis. I could not have succeeded without their help.

I also thank my research interviewees, who must remain nameless in accordance with standard research protocols. They know who they are and I want them to know I appreciate their time and commitment to my learning.

CONTENTS

FIRST PREFACE

Letters Patent: A Practical Theology of Work is a welcome contribution to the meagre Australian library section on the theology of work. Graham Leo has written a clear and concise theological reflection on human work from the heart of his experience as a committed Christian.

Graham had a personal 'wake-up moment' after retiring from his paid employment as a school principal after 25 years. He relates how, on the Sunday following his retirement, this significant transition event in his life was passed over without comment. He suddenly realised that this experience was common to all workers in his church. Graham imaginatively expresses the pain and sorrow of all workers, everywhere, around the church's failure to understand the vital connection between congregation members' faith and their experience of work.

Letters Patent gives voice to Graham's lament for this widespread loss from the church's failure to pray with workers at this time of life transition, and to fulfil its God-given mission to be in solidarity with the day-to-day working lives of its members.

Lament is the prayerful default of the biblical prophets in times of God's people's unfaithfulness. The prophets turn to God with the burden of their sorrow at the pain caused by the people's turning away from God, and they give voice to the truth of their people's suffering. Graham Leo's book gives voice to his prophetic truth about the Australian church's failure to minister to the working lives of its members, whether paid employment, voluntary work, housework or as carers. There is an urgency in his prophetic question, 'Will the church be up for the challenge?'

The sociological data does not give cause for hope. Graham briefly reports the National Church Life Survey (NCLS) data indicating the ageing and decline of Australian churches, before asking whether study of this data would make any difference to the way Parish Councils or similar bodies are operating. My observations, as a minister of the Uniting Church in Australia, reveal at the local, presbytery, state and national levels there is an almost wilful refusal to consider NCLS reports on work and faith. *Letters Patent* is the product of Graham's ten years study of the causes of the apparent reluctance, if not refusal, of Australian churches to intentionally engage with their members about their faith at work.

Graham's conclusions, grounded in his own experience of work and an extensive study of academic and popular theological literature on the subject, are an invitation to honest conversations within Australian churches. By my reading, Graham would be surprised if such conversations were initiated by clergy. The problem Graham has pinpointed is the hierarchy in Australian churches that values the work of ordained ministry as more spiritual than the secular work of lay people, whether paid or unpaid. In my ministry I met a number of men who had been encouraged by their minister to consider offering for ordained ministry, but who in each case told me they discerned that God was calling them to minister in a secular vocation. These men knew their call to a secular work was from God, and they reflected with me on how fruitful this calling was for them.

Paradoxically, I was struck by how often clergy who saw me regularly for pastoral supervision reported that they were 'stuck' in a struggle with the call of the church regarding their future in ordained ministry. They found their struggle resolved itself when I supported their return to their original call of Christ. For several of these ministers, remembering their original experience of the call of Christ on their lives liberated them to be open to new possibilities beyond the limiting parameters proposed by leaders of the institutional church. Graham seeks to encourage the church's return to a Reformation understanding of vocation, which values Christ's call to all people to discern their work for Christ's kingdom. *Letters Patent* is a very readable invitation to lay people to equip themselves theologically to see their work in this light, and by God's grace to bring their work and that of the church to greater fruitfulness.

Graham sheets the blame for the church's superiority complex about 'full-time Christian service' in the 'church-as-institution' to its inadequate theology of work – in particular, to the belief that work is cursed. His argument for this proposition is thoroughly biblical, and he draws on a range of popular Christian writers with whom I am not familiar. I believe Graham and I end up at a similar point, but arrive by different routes.

My view is that the Western culture that developed during the Enlightenment era dismissed Christianity as superstition, and so consigned faith to the private realm of subjective, irrational and emotional experience. At the same time, work that was rational, objective and scientifically based occupied the public world of economics and politics. A chasm developed between the spheres of private individual faith and public work 'in a world and society recalcitrant to the word-and-will of God'.

Perhaps where I differ from Graham is that he has more confidence that the matter of the world's recalcitrance to God's will may be addressed by improved theological/Christian education about work. However, Graham offers many useful suggestions for this improvement that are worthy of serious discussion. I commend leadership of this task at the local level to all who read *Letters Patent* and know they have been called to take up their 'vice-regal task' for the sake of God's kingdom.

John Bottomley
Director
Transforming Work
https://www.transformingwork.com.au
Member, Centre for Religion and Social Policy
University of Divinity (Melbourne)

SECOND PREFACE

Graham Leo's *Letters Patent: A Practical Theology of Work* lives up to its subtitle – it is profoundly practical. Rewritten in a user-friendly, snappy way from Graham's excellent and successful Doctor of Ministry thesis, which Neil Holm and I supervised, it is academically and theologically sound, without leaving the reader sound asleep.

Instead it seeks provocatively to wake the church up to the ever-present practical challenge of work and the apparent gap between Sunday church and Monday. Leo has 'skin in the game', having experienced that gap over many decades in his own work as a school principal. He relates how his work was largely ignored by his pastors and church. His hunch is that he is not alone in being anonymous and invisible as a worker in his church. Leo seeks, and largely succeeds, in making such workers, and their work, visible again.

The first chapter provides a brief but comprehensive busman's tour around the general world and theology of work – both current and historical. It provides a helpful panoramic perspective. He focuses on his research into whether regular church attendees have 'a clear understanding of what their work means in Christian terms'. Does it carry any value in God's kingdom? Do their ministers or their church as a whole, value and notice their work? Do their ministers see it as significant ministry or service? Do we 'work to live' or 'live to work'? In the view of Graham Leo, Dorothy Sayers and Alain de Botton, the ideal is the latter. Work is meant to be about dignity, meaning and thriving, not just surviving.

In the second chapter, *Some Real-Life Conversations about Work*, Leo provides a fly-on-the-wall insight into some revealing discussions with church-going workers. This puts some flesh onto the key topics the book addresses. He forgoes some of the 'methodological throat-clearing' of the academic thesis to get on with the well-constructed questions of his conversations. Some common themes showed up in comments and concerns regularly repeated by his interviewees, a small but reasonably representative sample of committed Christians with extensive experience of life in the church and in careers they valued and enjoyed. The first major theme that emerged was that of the recognition and valuing of work (a) by the interviewees and (b) by their churches. Needless to say, there was a big gap between their own positive evaluation of their work and their church's negative or non-existent evaluation.

Chapter 3 *Mondayitis and Thank God It's Friday!* addresses the important question of whether our human work is cursed. Leo argues that the common negativity regarding everyday work is grounded in the unconscious or default absorption (from both academic and popular theological sources) of the view that work is cursed – I once saw sloganised, 'Work – the curse of the drinking class!' Many would dispute this theoretically, but at a practical level actions speak louder than words.

In chapter 4, Leo counters this work-as-curse view, derived from Greek philosophical influences, by showing how a biblical view of work involves understanding what it means for human beings to be created *in imago Dei*. Genesis 1:26–28, known as the Creation or Cultural Commission sees work as a blessed expression of divinely delegated human 'dominion', but not domination, over the world.

This opens up the way to the major question of chapter 5: the notion of *calling* or *vocation*. Is the notion of calling only for ordained ministers as it was largely believed until the Reformation's rediscovery of the priesthood of all believers? Should we, as in my own Anglican Church, still have Vocations Days directed only to those considering ordination? Should the church's mission be seen primarily in terms of the calling of the ordained, rather than those on the frontlines of service/ ministry in daily work? In the Uniting Church, with its largely retired membership, daily work is largely ignored in the church's focus on its (albeit laudable) social justice ministries.

A further challenging of received categories is found in chapter 6: *How Can My Work Become Worship? A theology of work to take into your workplace or lifeplace.* Here Leo rightly highlights the biblical view stretching from Genesis 2:15 (describing work as *avodah* – service/worship) to Romans 12:1–2 where we are to present the work of our bodies and minds 'as a living sacrifice'. He explains how we ought to see daily work, paid or unpaid, as our true worship. (Another recent book in the recent renaissance of Australian work on this issue agrees; see *WorkShip: How To Use Your Work To Worship God* by Kara Martin.)

In a most useful and practical manner, Leo provides a range of practical recommendations in chapter 7. He provides a long list of suggestions for how the local church might engage with the work lives of their congregation members. This is followed by an Appendix: 'Calendar for Church Celebration of Workers and Work'. Would that every church would adopt such a calendar at the start of its year! If they did, the daily work of their congregations would no longer get squeezed out behind an array of ecclesiastical regalia and ritual.

The Australian church will be enriched if its many ordained

and lay leaders and everyday workers (paid or unpaid) *buy this book, study it in groups, and put into practice its recommendations.*

Rev'd Dr Gordon Preece
Director of RASP, University of Divinity Centre for Research in Religion and Social Policy
Director of Ethos: EA Centre for Christianity and Society
Minister of Yarraville Anglican Parish
Board Member of the Theology of Work Project
Author of numerous books on the theology and ethics of work

INTRODUCTION

In 2017 I completed a Doctor of Ministry degree. My research project investigated the ways in which a selection of Christians regarded their day-to-day work in terms of its kingdom significance, and also how the churches attended by those Christians regarded their work.

I have attended many different churches over four decades of adult Christian life, in many different places. None of them has taken any more than a passing interest in my work life. My research study set out to test whether my experience matched that of other church attenders.

In some ways, I have led a fortunate work life. I served as principal of two independent schools for a total of almost 25 years. One was a very large school, with over 1700 students and 250 staff. My work was recognised publicly and frequently. At the end of my career, when I retired, there were more ceremonies and honours than I can recall. Parents, students, staff, various professional associations, the community in general – they all offered their public and private thanks. I knew that my work was valued.

The only community with which I was closely associated that totally ignored my retirement from the world of paid work was my church! When I retired, as was equally true for anybody else in the church who ever retired, nothing happened. Nobody noted that a member of their community had ended a lifetime of work. For me that lack of recognition did not mean a great deal – though it surprised me – because I had been so generously feted within my school community over a period of many months. Truthfully, I was probably a bit over being farewelled – I didn't need another one. But it set me thinking. It made me wonder how a Christian who has spent a lifetime in work *no less meaningful than mine, but perhaps less publicly acknowledged at the end of it*, may feel at their retirement, or indeed during their working life.

Imagine a situation, perhaps not so likely in this mobile age: a person lives all their adult life in one city. They attend the same church for a large portion of their adult life. They spend their entire working life with one employer, perhaps as an accountant, a shoe salesperson, an optometrist, a truck-driver or a nurse. They retire after 45 years of working life, and go to church that first Sunday after their retirement party at work.

The church has a special focus that day on a new building project, or a mission in India, or the new way that they will be doing Home Groups from now on. Perhaps the minister announces the new year's theme: *Building Community through Relationships*, and shows a catchy video presentation. No-one mentions this massive change in their life. The person goes home, and feels somewhat … well … small.

Do people who attend church on Sunday just view the worship service as a time to forget about work? Is the church service a bit like Friday afternoon drinks – a time to put work out of your mind and just get on with the weekend until you have to turn up again on Monday morning?

Does an electrician, housewife or househusband, multinational CEO, surgeon, nurse, or carer of a disabled person ever get the sense that their church is interested in them as workers, or values their work as truly Christian service? Does their church reinforce in their minds that their day-to-day work has any value in itself, other than to provide money, some of which they can then give to their church?

Or does the advent of retirement after a lifetime of no

acknowledgement or engagement from their churches with them *as workers*, encourage retirees to climb into their caravans, or board their cruise ships, abandoning their work *vo*-cation for a life of perpetual *va*-cation as grey nomads?

Is it possible that our churches are blindly ignoring that single activity that absorbs the greater part of most people's attention for most of their lives? One National Church Life Survey recommended that churches nurture the relationship between the work lives and the church experience of members:

> Churches might consider the ways in which they can continue to foster a sense of collective identity and belonging for working people. This includes presenting a Christian understanding of the value and purpose of work, particularly for those who are not involved directly in ministry.[1]

This observation notes two tremendously important topics:

a. the development of a sense of identity and belonging for working people in the life of the church; and

b. teaching about the value and purpose of work.

In the last part of that quotation, however, it is impossible not to hear the probably unintentional trivialising of the work of most of us: 'particularly for those who are not involved directly in ministry'!

The workers chatting over their after-church coffee might feel pretty cheesed about that comment. *Who said my work as a doctor or carpenter or cleaner isn't at least as important as the work of that chap who's paid a lot of money just to play his guitar in his fashionably-torn jeans every Sunday morning?*

In my male experience, when the weekly church service is over, most men gather to discuss three common topics: their

---

[1] "Changes in Employment and Implications for Churches (2011)," NCLS Research, 2015, http://www.ncls.org.au/default.aspx?sitemapid=138.

previous week at work, sport and politics – often in that order. I don't know what women do, but I imagine that few discuss the sermon, the music, the announcements or the prayers that well-intentioned people laboured long over.

My experience reflects what Laura Nash described. She suggested there is a 'radical disconnection between Sunday services and Monday morning activities ... a sense of living in two worlds that never touch each other'.[2] This reflects what the Mennonite academic Calvin Redekop was quoted as saying:

> Most of us spend almost 40 per cent of our waking time at work. In contrast the average Christian spends less than 2 per cent (of his or her time) at church during their working years. Yet the church puts most of its energy into that 2 per cent; almost nothing into the world of work.[3]

Over many years, I have noted that when churches do address the topic of what it means to be a Christian at work, they nearly always address it in terms of how to be a more effective witness for Christ in the workplace. Every time I hear this sort of sermon, I have to admit that I cringe.

Quite apart from the fact that there is a thinly veiled encouragement to the congregation to steal their boss's time by evangelising their co-workers during their work time, this is surely the least-important aspect of what it means to be a Christian worker – that is, a worker who is a Christian. As Ian Hart wrote in 1995, sermons addressing the Christian value of day-to-day work are rare in church circles:

> In the author's experience sermons today rarely offer Christians any teaching or guidance about ordinary daily

---

2 Hugh Whelchel, *How Then Should We Work? Rediscovering the Biblical Doctrine of Work* (Bloomington, IN: WestBow Press, 2012), p. 70.

3 Alistair Mackenzie, "The Future for 'Faith at Work': A New Zealand Perspective," in *The Diaconal Church: Beyond the Mould of Christendom*, ed. David Clark (Peterborough, England: Fastprint Publishing, 2017), p. 72.

work, which in fact takes up the greater part of their time, energies and thinking. It was not always so. Luther, Calvin and the Puritan preachers spoke and wrote about the Christian's work regularly, comprehensively and perceptively.[4]

I want to include here a long quotation for two reasons: firstly, because it says what I want to say better than I can; and secondly, it comes from a book that deserves to be read much more widely than it currently is.

> In nothing has the Church so lost Her hold on reality as in Her failure to understand and respect the secular vocation. She has allowed work and religion to become separate departments ...
>
> How can anyone remain interested in a religion which seems to have no concern with nine-tenths of his life? The Church's approach to an intelligent carpenter is usually confined to exhorting him not to be drunk and disorderly in his leisure hours, and to come to church on Sundays. What the Church *should* be telling him is this: that the very first demand that his religion makes upon him is that he should make good tables. ...
>
> No crooked table legs or ill-fitting drawers ever, I dare swear, came out of the carpenter's shop at Nazareth. Nor, if they did, could anyone believe that they were made by the same hand that made Heaven and earth.
>
> No piety in the worker will compensate for work that is not true to itself; for any work that is untrue to its own technique is a living lie.[5]

Sayers has absolutely nailed this idea: Christian workers have

---

4 Ian Hart, "The Teaching of Luther and Calvin About Ordinary Work: 1. Martin Luther (1483–1546)," *Evangelical Quarterly* 67, no. 1 (1995): pp. 51–2.

5 Dorothy Sayers, *Letters to a Diminished Church* (New York: W Publishing Group, 2004), pp. 138-9.

to do excellent work. *That* is their Christian duty, not to try to evangelise their colleagues in company time. They should be recognised as the most reliable and trustworthy worker in the entire crew, office or staffroom, not the one who sends pithy little emails around their workplace with Bible texts or pithy sayings decorated with pretty angels and hearts, and amazing(!) Christian stories.

Sayers continues to hammer home her theme in her hard-hitting essay by pointing out that the only distinction between kinds of work is not whether the work is spiritual or secular; it is whether it is well done or shoddy.

> The official Church wastes time and energy, and, moreover, commits sacrilege, in demanding that secular workers should neglect their proper vocation in order to do Christian work – by which She means ecclesiastical work. ***The only Christian work is good work well done.*** Let the Church see to it that the workers are Christian people and do their work well, as to God: then all the work will be Christian work, whether it is church embroidery or sewage farming.[6]
> [Emphasis mine]

Years ago, my wife and I decided that we would no longer seek to hire Christian tradespersons to do work around our house. We had been disappointed too many times, delivered substandard work, forced to listen while they stood there (in the time we were paying for!) telling us about the latest Christian book they were reading, or why they couldn't finish our job because they were going to repair houses on the church mission trip to some Pacific island. We thought we would rather chance the rank ungodly to do our building repairs. We've generally been pretty happy with our decision.

Between the National Church Life Survey and Dorothy Sayers, it seemed to me that there was a good deal of work

---

6 Ibid., 140.

to be done on improving the way that churches and their members regarded their work. This book is a summary of some of the research I conducted – my original research and also my gleanings from the research of others from poring over the literature. This little book represents well over a decade of study, reading and thinking.

The original thesis was, of course, written in an academic style of writing. I've tried to change the style of writing here to a more popular style, to make the book more widely accessible. I don't mean that the content is dumbed down. On the contrary, I really hope that it will stretch many readers. I have tried to avoid too much academic jargon, and too many complicated constructions. You will have to be the judge on whether I have succeeded at this.

I have, however, maintained a large number of academic references, and a substantial bibliography in order to assist anyone who might want to investigate these topics further in a more academic study. There are many aspects of this area that should be researched further, especially in the Australian context.

Another reason that I chose to write in a popular style, rather than produce an academic tome, is this. In my thesis, I levelled a serious criticism at the many popular books I read in my literature research. My criticism was that popular writing on this topic almost uniformly repeats at least one wrong foundational principle. This compounded error has, in my view, been very detrimental to the thinking of Christians across the world regarding their day-to-day work.

This book attempts to correct that failure in the popular literature. I am not unaware of my own temerity in daring to do this. I ask my readers to be patient and gracious with me. I am not a professional theologian, though I have studied theology. I am not an ordained minister, though I have preached hundreds, possibly thousands of sermons. I am a schoolteacher, a reader, a writer and a worker.

I hope that I might approach the status of what Alister McGrath calls an 'organic theologian' – an ordinary Christian who believes the Bible to contain the true word of God, and who attempts to understand it well and communicate its truth to others. McGrath suggests that the organic theologian should:

> … see himself as working within the great historical Christian tradition, which he gladly makes his own. Even when he feels he must critique the contemporary expressions or applications of that tradition, he will do so from a deep commitment to the community of faith and its distinctive ideas and values. He will not see his task as imposing alien ideas upon his community, but as being like the householder who brings out of his treasures 'things new and old' (Mt 13:52).[7]

It is my prayer that this book will advance the cause of Christ and his church, by improving and enlightening the ways that Christian churches and Christian workers engage with one another in their common cause of worshipping together and working together.

---

[7] Alister McGrath, *The Future of Christianity* (Oxford: Blackwell Publishers, 2002), p. 152.

CHAPTER ONE
Work to Live or Live to Work?

Setting the scene for thinking about work

Mark Twain is reputed to have said: 'Work and play are words used to describe the same thing under differing conditions.' Dorothy Sayers declared that 'work is not, primarily, a thing one does to live, but the thing one lives to do.'[1]

Judging by how most people talk about work in their casual moments, we could assume that work is something you do in order to earn money. We work in order to live. Work is something you escape from as soon as you can, in order to do something you like doing. We make jokes about it: *I like work – I could watch it all day long.* Tradesmen drive around in cars with bumper stickers saying, 'I'd rather be fishing.'

Recent Australian research on how workers view their work, however, indicates that workers are rather more serious about their work than these casual comic quips suggest. In a study[2] that examined what Australians regard as *their most important sources of peace and wellbeing,* what rated most highly was 'spending time with family and friends' (89% of respondents). 'Relaxing – doing nothing at all' (53%) and 'Working' (52%) were, however, almost equally valued. Surprisingly, for an Australian study, 'watching sport' rated only 23%, just marginally ahead of 'attending church services' at 21%, demonstrating that Australians highly value the work aspect of their lives.

[1] Sayers, *Letters to a Diminished Church*, pp. 134-5.

[2] John Bellamy et al., *Why People Don't Go to Church* (Adelaide, SA: Openbook Publishers, 2002), p. 44.

These results are at odds with the fairly dismal view of work often presented on TV and in comedies. Work genuinely seems to be integral to what it means to be human.

Men and women at work

There's an old joke that when men are working, for example, on roadwork sites, they have to put up a sign saying so: *Men at Work*. Women don't need to do that, because they are always working.

In only the last 30 years or so, across all developed nations, the world of work has undergone a massive adjustment. Women have entered the paid workforce in large numbers. More importantly, women have come to view paid work, outside the home, as their fundamental right. We should not underplay the historical significance of this.

Men and women have historically regarded work differently, at least since the advent of the industrial revolution. We have had 200 years of men working outside the home, and women working inside the home. For whatever reasons, our society came to value these two kinds of work very differently. Of course, I am not suggesting it was either right or wise to do so. But the fact is that we did. It is important to trace this development.

Work became, for men, a form of self-actualisation. Their work generally took place outside of the family home, in places where they had to make their own way, establish their own reputation. This produced attitudes towards work very different from those in the rural village, where every man worked his own little farm or small business.

Once work became identified as 'that thing that you do when you leave the house', and 'that thing that all men do once they have grown up', it became a duty. No man worthy of the name would be without a job. To be unemployed meant to be less than a man.

Furthermore, your work was something you did on your own. On the farm, in the village, your family all chipped in to help in various ways. If you were really in trouble, the neighbours might have offered help. Work outside the home and village became the lonely road that every man had to travel to make his way on his own. A boy's work 'made a man' out of him.

Teachers, uncles, and, of course, parents, all started to talk to young boys about what they would 'be' when they grew up. It was no longer enough to reply: 'I'll be honest and good and kind.' A boy had to become a carpenter or a doctor or a teacher or a soldier.

Everybody understood, until quite recently, that girls would become wives and housewives, but boys had to become *Something*! My wife went to secondary school in the 1960s, but her post-war European migrant father told her that she could not do Year 11 and 12 because she was a girl and would just get married. Education would be wasted on her. It was only when she earned a scholarship to stay at school for those final two years that he relented.

We were married in 1971, and were both teachers. Had she been married just a year or so earlier, she would have had to resign her job as a teacher in the State Education Department as soon as she married. By then, she was allowed to keep her job, but I was paid more than she was because I was a man.

Men's work developed a greater value than women's work because it was externalised from ordinary home life. This could never have happened in an agriculturally-based environment. Pittman put it bluntly: 'Men have been specialized and trained to sacrifice their emotions and even their lives for what they have been told is their duty as men. Men have been given few choices: men work.'[3]

---

[3] Frank Pittman, *Man Enough: Fathers, Sons, and the Search for Masculinity*

The protagonist of Joseph Conrad's classic *Heart of Darkness* declared: 'I don't like work – no man does – but I like what is in the work – the chance to find yourself. Your own reality – for yourself, not for others – what no other man can ever know.'[4]

The popular television drama *The West Wing* portrayed men's high regard for their own work, even well into the 21st century (Leo McGarry is the White House Chief of Staff in this dialogue with his wife, Jenny):

> Leo: *This is the most important thing I'll ever do, Jenny. I have to do it well.*
>
> Jenny: *It's not more important than your marriage.*
>
> Leo:...*It is more important than my marriage, right now. These few years while I'm doing this, yes, it's more important than my marriage.*[5]

This process of self-authentication through work has deeply marked the way we view all work, but especially paid work. The social revolution for women in paid work is still young, historically speaking, and we should be cautious about being too dogmatic about how women will come to regard their paid work in coming decades. Nevertheless, it seems fairly likely that many women will come to regard paid work as having the same kind of self-authenticating role that it is perceived that men's work has had. We are probably not yet at that point, however, at least not in Christian circles.

Barna research conducted in 2018 reported that:

working moms (compared with fathers, single men and single women) are well behind on all metrics of satisfaction—

(New York: Perigee Press, 1993), p. 10.

4 Joseph Conrad, *Heart of Darkness* (Claremont CA: Coyote Canyon Press, 2007), 38.

5 Aaron Sorkin et al., "The West Wing the Complete Series," (Directed by Michael Lehmann, Warner Home Video, 2006), Episode 104.

relational, spiritual, emotional, you name it. Their attitudes toward vocation also differ.

For instance, even though both mothers and fathers share an equal desire to use their gifts and talents for the good of others (64% and 62%), mothers feel significantly less called to or made for their current work than fathers (38% compared to 55%).

Moms and dads share an equal desire to use their gifts and talents for the good of others, but working mothers feel significantly less called to their current work than fathers (38% and 55%).[6]

Whether this is a good thing, or whether work has actually been so effective at authenticating men's inner selves, seems to go largely unexamined. It is a truism generally that unemployment is regarded as being destructive to any person's self-respect. The more 'fulfilling' one's work can be, however, the better it is for one's general wellbeing.

From the point of view of churches, one would think that the world of work – since it deals so closely with how people regard their true selves and their social 'value' – would have been of great interest. After all, this is what churches are focused on: the essential selves and the spiritual value of human beings.

John Bottomley's candid confession of his time as a parish minister demonstrates what may be true of many Australian churches: 'Men were largely invisible to me because most of them were in paid employment.'[7] As Bottomley observed, apart from the money earned at work that workers give to support the church, the paid work of parishioners often has 'little or no

---

6 "Christians at Work: Examining the Intersection of Calling and Career," ed. Roxanne Stone (Ventura, CA: Barna Group, 2018).

7 John Bottomley, *Hard Work Never Killed Anybody: How the Idolisation of Work Sustains This Deadly Lie* (Northcote, VIC: Morning Star Publishing, 2015), p. 11.

consequence for the mission of the church'.[8]

As early as 1987, Peter Kaldor commented that: 'the concerns and experiences of those in the workplace must become an important issue for the churches.'[9] If people experience a disconnection between their daily life and church life, and if churches generally do not recognise that disconnection nor attempt to address it, it is likely to increase over time.

A failure to address this disconnection is likely to result in a growing sense of irrelevance of the church experience, and a decrease in their frequency of attendance. This reflects what we know to be the actual, current case with regard to church attendance across all developed nations, even if we have not established a causal connection.

The film *The Full Monty*[10] featured a man who had been made redundant from his job. Too embarrassed to reveal the truth of his redundancy to his wife, he dressed in his suit every morning and left the house, not returning home until after 5.00 p.m. This real-life deception has become so well known that it frequently features in television sitcoms and dramas.[11]

It is surely axiomatic that part of the local church's mission is to seek to meet the deepest human needs in a local community. If our daily work is so intimately related to our sense of personal being and worth, and if, when we do attend church, our work is so marginalised or ignored that it is made to appear virtually

---

8 Ibid.

9 Peter Kaldor, *Who Goes Where? Who Doesn't Care?* (Homebush West, NSW: Lancer, 1987), p. 107.

10 Peter Cattaneo, "The Full Monty," (UK: Fox Searchlight, 1997).

11 'What do you do when you are married to the job, and the job dumps you? Many breadwinners, almost always male, derive most of their sense of self-worth and achievement from their ability to bring home the bacon. The flip side is that getting laid off can deal a devastating blow to their self-esteem, and they may conceal the fact from their wife and kids, sometimes for months.' "TV Tropes," http://tvtropes.org/pmwiki/pmwiki.php/Main/UnconfessedUnemployment cited January, 2016.

irrelevant to our faith-life, then it would be hardly surprising if we came to think that it was simply not worth our while to attend church.

Churches used to have to think only about *men* at work – hence the missions to sailors, chaplains in the army, and soup kitchens for unemployed men. It is highly doubtful whether churches ever seriously understood what men's work was all about. It is even less likely (given their male-centred leadership structures) that they have even begun to comprehend the massive social change in women's work.

Finding truly human meaning in work

In Alain de Botton's charming reflection on contemporary work, *The Pleasures and Sorrows of Work*, he describes the work of an artist:

> How different everything is for the craftsman who transforms a part of the world with his own hands ... and see[s] it as a stable repository of his skills and an accurate record of his years, and hence feel[s] collected together in one place ... [He] knows he is creating things which exceed him.[12]

In contrast to such apparently meaningful work, de Botton describes in close detail the work of many people in apparently dull, repetitive jobs, such as production lines in factories. Such jobs do not readily provide a clear sense of purpose or meaning for those who perform them.

De Botton describes some unpaid activities that most of us would probably find less than interesting, such as 'container ship spotting' or the fascinating activities of a member of the Pylon Appreciation Society.[13] He draws no major distinction

---

12 Alain de Botton, *The Pleasures and Sorrows of Work* (London: Penguin, 2010), p. 182.

13 Members of this unusual social club travel vast distances to admire, study and be near huge electricity pylons.

between these voluntary activities and paid work, regardless of whether they suit all of us or not. They are all human activity. This will be an important perspective to remember when we eventually get to a definition of work.

De Botton's forensic examination of and reflection on work from his self-declared atheistic perspective was fascinating (and enjoyable) for me to read, as a Christian. He describes the continual search for meaningful connections between people's activity/work and their essential humanity as essentially a spiritual quest.

The church, as the body of Christ, ought to be a place for Christians to reasonably expect to find such connections. As Peel noted, 'When we work to meet legitimate human needs, we are working for God and God is working through us, whether we realize it or not.'[14] Too often the typical Sunday church service and the normal round of church activities do not encourage us to relate to them through the filter of our daily work.

What is work?

In chapter Four, we will look in detail at what work is, from a biblical point of view. But we should at least start thinking about it now, even if we might adjust our ideas later, when we know a little more than we know now.

It is astonishingly difficult to find a simple definition of work that covers all its parts. It is a human activity performed by people of virtually all ages from early childhood onwards, an activity that may be paid, unpaid, voluntary or coerced, and

---

14 Bill Peel, "Does Your Work Matter in God's Eyes?," Centre for Faith and Work, LeTourneau University, http://www.centerforfaithandwork. com/node/729?utm_source=MMM+1st+August+Send+8/10/15&utm_ campaign=MMM+1st+Aug+email+8/10/15&utm_medium=email cited 8 Feb., 2016.

which may or may not bring any sense of satisfaction to the doer.

The range of views offered in the following widely differing definitions of work provided by Christian writers demonstrates this complexity:

> *Work is what weaves together the very fabric of a called person's identity, and fulfils it.*[15] (We will examine this vexed question of 'calling' in Chapter Five.)

> *Work can be defined as human activity that has both intrinsic and extrinsic value; that involves physical and emotional energy; that can be both tedious and exhilarating; and that often is done out of necessity and in exchange for financial remuneration but also is done out of joy and in return for self-fulfilment and accomplishment.*[16]

> *Work is honest, purposeful ... social activity whose primary goal is the creation of products or states of affairs that can satisfy the needs of working individuals or their co-creatures, ... activity that is necessary in order for acting individuals to satisfy their needs apart from the need for the activity itself.*[17]

Other descriptions of work from a Christian perspective include references to 'work undertaken to the glory of God',[18] or to almost any activity that involves the expenditure of effort,[19]

---

15 Ben Witherington, III, *Work: A Kingdom Perspective on Labor* (Grand Rapids, MI: William B. Eerdmans, 2011), p. 13.

16 David W. Miller, *God at Work: The History and Promise of the Faith at Work Movement* (New York: Oxford University Press, 2007), p. 19.

17 Miroslav Volf, *Work in the Spirit: Toward a Theology of Work* (Eugene, OR: Wipf and Stock Publishers, 2001), p. 10.

18 Witherington, *Work*, p. xii.

19 *Work means any activity by man, whether manual or intellectual, whatever its nature or circumstances; it means any human activity that can and must be recognized as work.* John Paul II, Laborem Exercens (on Human Work): Encyclical Letter of the Supreme Pontiff on Human Work, (Vatican1981), http://w2.vatican.va/content/john-paul-ii/en/encyclicals/documents/hf_jp-ii_enc_14091981_laborem-exercens.html 1.

and sometimes note the inclusion of 'unpaid and domestic work'.[20] Gomez concluded that as a society, we actually have no clear definition of work.[21]

Scripture is replete with examples of intellectual or artistic work that is honoured. Consider, for example, Joseph's gifts of administration, Jethro's advice to Moses, musical works in the Psalms and so on. Jethro was not an Israelite, either; he was a Midianite priest, which may have relevance for how we think about the work of non-believers. God's 'calling' of Bezalel and Oholiab to the task of construction and artistic decoration of the tabernacle is frequently cited as an example of 'sacred' work.[22]

Christians and non-believers come from two opposing world views, to arrive at almost identical destinations, where work occupies a central place in the life of human beings.

The popular atheist, Alain de Botton, whose writing we looked at above, suggested that work possesses an 'extraordinary claim to be able to provide us, alongside love, with the principal source of life's meaning'.[23] This atheist's insight may be closer to Christian theology than much popular Christian writing that seems to have been written in complete ignorance of Dorothy Sayers' observations.

Dorothy Sayers, whose writing we have already extensively

---

20 Gordon R. Preece, *The Viability of the Vocation Tradition in Trinitarian, Credal and Reformed Perspective: The Threefold Call* (New York: The Edwin Mellen Press, 1998), p. 301.

21 'As a society, we do not seem to have any clear sense of what work is, what work is for, and how the work of the individual is related to the work of others.' Jose H. Gomez, "All You Who Labor: Towards a Spirituality of Work for the 21st Century," (2006), http://scholarship.law.nd.edu/ndjlepp/vol20/iss2/11. p. 792.

22 The phrase used of this manual, technical task, 'to devise skilful works' (Ex 35:32) might be literally translated as 'to think thoughts'. J. H. Hertz, ed. *Pentateuch and Haftorahs* (London: Soncino Press, 1960), p. 375.

23 de Botton, *The Pleasures and Sorrows of Work*, p. 30.

quoted, claimed that work should be regarded, 'not as a necessary drudgery to be undergone for the purpose of making money, but as a way of life in which the nature of man might find its proper exercise and delight and so fulfil itself to the glory of God'.[24]

The philosopher Michael Oakeshott drew a thoughtful distinction between play and work that has, perhaps, not been sufficiently considered: 'Philosophy, science, and history are, then, activities that belong not to "work" but to "play".'[25] The approach to work that I will develop in this book will attempt to draw the secular and Christian world views of work (and play) closer together.

The changing nature of work in the 21st century

Two centuries of the effects of the Industrial and Information Revolutions have resulted in society and the workplace showing signs of stress.[26] The close relationship between work and a person's identity that I argued for above is acknowledged as a major issue, even in 'secular' publications, as we enter a new era of work:

> Work... the thing that *provided* – that allowed families to prosper and individuals to build a sense-of-self – is under attack. ... work is so deeply ingrained into our very identity. Even when work is degrading and miserable, we still associate it with self-reliance, self-realization and something redemptive.[27]

---

24 Sayers, *Letters to a Diminished Church*, p. 125.

25 Michael Oakeshott, "Work and Play," *First Things* June/July (1995), http://www.firstthings.com/article/2008/09/003-work-and-play-15

26 For a longer discussion of this, see Roman Krznaric, *How to Find Fulfilling Work* (London: Macmillan, 2012), p. 6.

27 Ben Schiller, "Welcome to the Post-Work Economy," 15 March (2016), http://www.fastcoexist.com/3056483/welcome-to-the-post-work-economy.

Employers sometimes complain about young people who show no loyalty to a career or an employer, and who see themselves as doing their employer a favour by working for them.[28] The old industrial models of workers who report to a boss and obediently follow instructions are giving way to new models of greater cooperation, emphasising the role of teams in effective work.[29]

The West is facing rapid social change, including how we work.[30] The church in all its varied forms must respond with changes in how it operates.[31] Some of the employment-related changes that are likely to have an effect on the ways that people relate to church, and how churches relate to their people, include the following:

- *Shrinkage of available free time:* People are spending more time at work than ever before, especially when long city commutes are taken into account. Many churches are finding it harder to attract their congregations to midweek or Saturday activities. Where once, attending morning and evening Sunday services weekly was not regarded as especially abnormal, attendance once every three weeks is now regarded as 'regular' by most churches, and by research bodies.

28 Louis White, "Why Aren't Gen Y Satisfied?," *Sydney Morning Herald* 17 May, 2016.

29 'Today's teams are different from the teams of the past; they're far more diverse, dispersed, digital, and dynamic (with frequent changes in membership).' Martine Haas and Mark Mortensen, "The Secrets of Great Teamwork," *Harvard Business Review* June (2016): p. 71.

30 Barna draws comparisons between social change and changes needed in churches, in George Barna, *Revolution* (Carol Stream, IL: Tyndale House, 2005).

31 Mark L. Russell, "The Secret of Marketplace Leadership Success: Constructing a Comprehensive Framework for the Effective Integration of Leadership, Faith, and Work," *Journal of Religious Leadership* 6, no. 1 (2007): p. 77.

- *Decreasing job security:* Employers are moving to greater on-demand, freelance services, away from traditional salaried employees. They are increasingly utilising their 'rapidly expanding non-employee workforce' and increasing 'their use of independent talent'.[32] This work is typically then performed at home, at times to suit the worker. One estimate is that 33% of Australia's workforce is engaged in freelance work, while for the particular age group known as millennials, 42% are so engaged.[33] This sense of being 'temporary' or 'transitory' or 'mobile' feeds into the notion of not being committed to anything, including church. Sunday morning might be a lovely quiet time to work!

- *The Gig Economy:* Younger workers are moving in droves into working short-term contracts or one-off tasks rather than seeking permanent work. Some of these jobs are done for people they will never meet. They are searched for and responded to, via the internet; remuneration is offered and accepted online; once the task is done and sent to the owner digitally, payment is made electronically. Your work could be done by a person on the other side of the world, or in the next-door office – and you may not even know. It may even be done while at their day-job pretending to be doing the work of their primary boss, who is also paying them for their time.

---

32 Jeff Wald, "Five Predictions for the Freelance Economy in 2016," *Forbes* 9 December (2015), http://www.forbes.com/sites/waldleventhal/2015/12/09/5-predictions-for-the-freelance-economy-in-2016/#357c631d63d7.
33 "Australia's Freelance Economy Grows to 4.1 Million Workers, Study Finds," *The Indian Telegraph* 27 October (2015), http://theindiantelegraph.com.au/australias-freelance-economy-grows-to-4-1-million-workers-study-finds/

- *Variable geographic location:* We are accustomed to people working from home for part of their employed time, but a greater shift in workplace culture now sees workers sharing temporary, rent-by-the-hour space.[34] This is an urban version of remote fly-in, fly-out workers.

- *The effects of artificial intelligence (AI) on the availability of jobs:* Relatively simple automation erased about 8 million jobs in the USA in the first decade of this century.[35] Artificial intelligence could make those job losses seem paltry within the next two decades.

- *A decreasing sense of loyalties:* Senior administrators and CEOs have traditionally been used to having permanent work, while hiring temporary office staff according to need. There is now a well-established practice of hiring even CEOs on a temporary basis.[36] Churches with strong traditional heritages, providing a sense of long-term stability, may find that they have something that more modern, free-moving churches cannot. Knowing how to capitalise on that asset, however, is likely to elude those traditional churches who may not even be aware of it.

---

34 Howarth reported on a facility in Melbourne called The Village 'where up to 100 small-business customers can work at any one time. More than 500 customers have become members … along with a further 370 businesses and community partners … that would not otherwise have access to a similar space in the city.' Brad Howarth, "Future of Work: How Nab and Microsoft Are Creating Tomorrow's Workplace Today," *Business Review Weekly* 14 April (2014), http://www.brw.com.au/p/leadership/future_workplace_work_today_nab_xd7t3IlKb0SMrBHVecFi9H.

35 John Lancaster, "Leveling the Playing Field," *Time* February 4–11 (2019): p. 76.

36 Jody Greenstone and Matt Miller, "The Rise of the Supertemp," *Harvard Business Review* May (2012), https://hbr.org/2012/05/the-rise-of-the-supertemp.

- *Never being away from work:* Increased reliance on personal technology devices results in workers feeling that they are 'always turned-on and can't ever completely shut off from work'.[37]

- *A move away from salaried work to a government-provided Universal Basic Income,[38] with people doing freelance work to supplement that income as they choose:* It is likely that the next half-century will see changes to the working environment of people, at least in advanced countries,[39] that create paradigm shifts that have as much impact on the world of work as the creation of the printing press, or the industrial and information revolutions.[40]

As these societal changes take effect, workers and churches will need to adapt. The concept of being at work from 9.00 to 5.00 Monday to Friday, turning up at church for a working bee on Saturday and then again to worship on Sunday, is ripe for renewal.

This old model relies on a more or less stable membership, living and working in predictable and stable ways and times, with work pressures located safely away from Sunday morning, and weekends in general. Such a society may already be consigned to a past never to be retrieved. Will the church be up for the challenge?

---

37 "State of Work in Australia," (Reventure, in association with Barna, 2016).
38 Nick Srnicek and Alex Williams, *Inventing the Future: Postcapitalism and a World without Work* (London: Verso Books, 2015). This idea is actually almost a century old but is only now starting to gain traction. It would significantly alter the way we think about money and work.
39 Trials are already under way in several advanced countries (e.g. Finland, Switzerland and Sweden) of a UBI system. Schiller, "Welcome to the Post-Work Economy".
40 Paul Mason, *Postcapitalism: A Guide to Our Future* (London: Penguin, 2016).

Summary

In this chapter, I have tried to take a brief but comprehensive tour around the general world of work – both now and in the past. The purpose was to start thinking about work in ways that we may not have done, before now.

In my research, I decided to focus on trying to find out whether people who attend church regularly have a clear understanding of what their work means in Christian terms. Does it have any value in the kingdom of God? I also wanted to find out whether they perceived that their church leaders, or their church in general, took any serious account of them as workers.

In the following chapter, I will give a very brief insight into some of the conversations that I recorded in my interviews with the participants in my research group. I've done this, early on in the book, to put some 'flesh' on the topics we will be talking about.

The words of real people who were willing to talk about themselves and their work should prepare our minds and hearts to delve deeply into what this thing called work really is.

CHAPTER TWO
Some Real-Life Conversations about Work

Excerpts from my research conversations

My research showed up some common themes – comments and opinions that were repeated over and again by most of my interviewed participants. All of them were sincere and committed Christians, with a long experience of life in the church, and all were in careers that they valued and enjoyed.

The participants included (in part), a lawyer, a high-level medical researcher, a school Principal, a house-builder, a digital marketing business owner, a chiropractor, a medical specialist, a national CEO of a not-for-profit charity, and a project manager of a private corporation specialising in large construction. They came from most major Christian denominations, both Protestant and Catholic.

A theme was regarded to have emerged if it was clearly expressed or endorsed by at least 80% of my interviewees. Many were expressed unanimously, or nearly so. Where there was a significant outlier, I identified that – but these were actually quite rare.

I have chosen to use direct quotations from the participants in my research group, to allow their real voices to be heard. I have made only occasional minor textual changes to cover gaps or make links within a longer response for greater comprehension. Additions in square brackets are provided by me for the purpose of clarification.

Each separate paragraph in each section is generally a different participant's voice, within that subheading.

Of course, this is only a very small selection of the entire research project. I've covered here just three of the six themes, as these relate most closely to the content of this book.

Major Theme One: the recognition and valuing of work (a) by the participant and (b) by their church

Subtheme: I believe that my own work has real value in the kingdom of God.

Well, I think what we do has an impact on society. There are 20–25 people that come to work in our business. They have jobs, they get to send their kids to school; they get to pay their bills; they get to do that and do things that they enjoy, and make them feel good – and that's a good thing!

I think that for people to do their professions to the best of their ability, as long as they're productive and helpful things to mankind in general … then I'm doing that.

Oh absolutely! I would say absolutely. In terms of building the kingdom of God, yes. Absolutely!

Absolutely! I think that… I have no scriptural background for this view other than a general gist of theology, but I think some of the stuff we learn in this life we get to carry on into the next. And so, I think, in the next, well it's not the next life, because technically, we're in the life, we're saved, we have life. It's in the next body, in the next dimension, it's in eternity once this earth has gone, I think we're carrying through, we're gonna learn new ways of doing things. There's gonna be city planners, there's gonna be engineers, and there's gonna be commerce and there's gonna be trade. We're gonna have to build buildings and I think we're gonna get a chance to do lots of cool things, so I think if we all turned up as ministers,… I think maybe the ministers are the ones who'll be redundant in the next life!

My Christian life and my work are both about making good use of my life; about doing something that's purposeful, about honouring God, about serving God, about using my time on this earth, short as it is, to some effect. … Two ways I can think of immediately. One is, that I'm modelling an approach personally to doing research and to thinking about the world and acting on that research in a manner which leads to application of findings for public health. I'm hoping that for the next generation of public researchers, I'm modelling an approach that takes a Christian world view which is logical, respectful, honouring of God, honest, with virtue and integrity … and making, through my group, our own small and increasing number of contributions to improving the public health.

Oh absolutely! … My conviction is that it's part of the redemptive story. I don't necessarily see how it's part of that redemptive story, I have to take that by faith. But nevertheless I am called to re-imagine my work, not just as a means to an end, but as an essential element of being obedient to my Lord; to believe and to trust that he will take what is offered by faith and somehow weave it into the fabric of his big redemptive story. … The incarnation says that he takes our humanity, what we do from day to day, <u>that</u> seriously, it would seem to me to be kicking sand in our Creator's face, not to value what I do when I turn up on Monday morning.

Subtheme: I don't see any evidence that my church values, recognises or seriously takes note of my day-to-day work, or my work skills, in any significant way, if at all.

I definitely felt a very strong sense of rejection from the church, [in regards to my professional skills] rightly or wrongly.

I don't want to mow the lawns, and I can't learn songs to play the guitar, so I'm quite happy to turn up to a committee. ... But... I think if you put your professional rate on those activities and said 'OK. Would you be prepared to pay me $1200 to turn up to this meeting?', I reckon they'd darned well run it in less than half an hour, and provide pre-reading and minutes and genuine Action Items. To stretch it out for six hours is just ... I think the church devalues the people they've got in their pews.

I asked one of the ministers of my church, 'I see you've advertised for elders; can you tell me what an elder is, what the definition of an elder is, in this church?' and their response was, 'Oh you'd be a really good elder, perhaps in a year or two's time when you've really found your feet.' I thought, what does finding one's feet entail? ... So there was no understanding of who I was, what roles I'd played in the past, what I could bring to this organisation, this church.

So very often I feel that those things, those skills, are completely under-utilised. ... I don't think my skills are well utilised. I think sometimes churches don't see their members as real people with real jobs and skills, just as church members.

Umm... I don't think so. I think at a parish level, they actually see my work and their environment as quite different.

My skills are not really being exercised in that context at the moment. Other than in conversations I might have with the people of God either side of the gathered worship. However, they are probably being offered privately, and in the mystery of faith corporately, as I participate in corporate worship. Perhaps also simply by the life of prayer, in my personal response, through the declarations of faith that are being made, through the thankfulness for insight and epiphany that comes during the gathered worship.

Subtheme: *I don't see any evidence that my church sees my daily work as service in the kingdom of God.*

I think if you were to ask them [i.e. my church leaders] *that question, they would have said, 'Definitely, yes!'. But not really. Not in practice.*

If you measured that in share of voice, I mean, do they talk about it on a Sunday morning to the church community, in comparison to the share of voice gained by missionaries in the mission field, or pastors in pastor training, or any of the traditional Christianese type of things, then you'd have to say it's about 0.2% airtime.

I don't think anyone has ever consciously thought about it, to be honest. I don't think that the church actually perceives that. … But as a church the answer would probably be 'No.'

No, I don't think so, It's not good at empowering someone like me to see it as God's work, you know, to get someone like me out the front and interview me like this, like we're doing now, would be great, so that other people would see that, you know, that... [After a very long silence where I could see that he was struggling for words, and had lapsed into a thoughtful reverie, I gently prompted him with: *That my work matters?* He instantly replied:] *Yeah, that my work matters! That there is a God-mindedness about the way I go about things. It has done that sometimes but rarely, you know, rarely.* [I felt that this last sentence was spoken with a deep sadness in the voice. Our interview paused for quite a few moments, as he recovered his emotions before we could go on.]

Umm. You know, I've probably never had that sense.

One of my participants was attending two different churches at the time, and replied thus: *Look, I think both do, certainly the 'XYZ' Church does, but probably both seek to do so, or at least would desire to do so. However, there still seems to me to be a major disconnect between what is emphasised in the life of the church and what we do from Monday to Friday. It's as if what we do from Monday to Friday is not part of the life of the church. It's separate from. So although there's the sense of the body of Christ both gathered and dispersed, it's still the being-the-church-in-action in both those contexts that is not held and maintained well by churches in general.*

Subtheme: Sermons on work or teaching on work are rarely if ever presented at my church.

Not on a weekly basis – but certainly, there have been many instances where people, preachers and teachers, have reflected on how one would go out and behave and act throughout the whole week, be changed, inspired, by what's been discussed on Sunday.

Hmmm. (Long pause) This is going to sound terrible but not without the context of appealing to the rich. I'm sounding really cynical, but when the topic is addressed, it's addressed under the guise, of "Oh, so we also have this building campaign," or "Oh, by the way, we want to launch this." I mean, I'm a pretty good communicator and I know how to run a communications campaign. So when you see it in action, you can see right through it. So when the focus shifts to that topic, … 9.9 times out of ten, it is invariably followed up with, "Put your hand in your pocket." So in my view, that's what probably leaves a bad taste in your mouth.

When I thought about that, you know I can't actually place a particular sermon, or say that I have ever heard a sermon devoted to work. I can certainly think of many examples where something has been preached about, and then elements of that as practical implementation in the workplace have been alluded to or spoken about. You know, how do we take this, how do we make use of that in the workplace.

How is your work important? I could count on one hand the number of times in 30 years that I've heard a sermon addressing that question.

Ahhh, I've probably given one or two. (laughter) But no, not directly about work …

I pondered that before I came, and I actually came up with one sermon I could think of, and it was related to a book that came out, I think it was 2005. [I prompted: *We're talking here of 20 years or more of going to church?* He replied,] *Yes.*

Well, yes. Perhaps not very often, but perhaps in the context of a series on stewardship, I would've heard sermons about our work as being important, and what we do on a day-to-day basis as being a significant thing. But not very often … Maybe once a year. Perhaps on the stewardship Sunday or something like that.

Other observations that arose from questions asked in the context of this theme revealed that not one of my research interviewees had ever attended a local church where there was a regular, at-least-annual service when the working lives of members would be prayed for. Several mentioned that that kind of thing sometimes happened in regard to the starting of a new year when all the Sunday School teachers and youth workers would be prayed for, but never for 'secular' workers. One mentioned a city cathedral church where the church prayed, in a special annual service, *for all the workers employed by that church in its own various ministries* across the state.

Major Theme Two: the question of vocation and sacred-secular distinctions

[In response to the prompt: So full-time Christian service is commonly regarded as more important than secular work?]:

Absolutely! Absolutely! That was very much part of the culture that I grew up in. I had a lot of friends and relatives that were spread across a whole heap of different denominations and backgrounds, and I would say without a doubt, that was a very universal thought that was held across – not just in my own church – but was part of the Christian culture that I grew up in.

[In response to the same prompt]: *I would say that is the conception, the accepted position, consistently.*

[In response to the same prompt]: *That's probably my experience, that people who can sing and preach, and, you know, bring those kinds of upfront gifts, and ministry to the church, are the ones who are valued. The secular gifts as we call them, like how to run a business effectively, or how to have correct procedures in an organisation, probably aren't valued.*

I think that there's equal value between what we're doing out in society to what a church is doing. I'm not saying it's more or less. I'm just saying equivalent.

When people stand up in church and talk about how they gave up their career to go into ministry … I think they are devaluing by that kind of statement everything that everybody else does as workers in the church. Because yes, there's no doubt that there is a calling, and I understand that people make sacrifices when they go to the mission field. I don't want to devalue what happens on any platform in any church, but I think that it's almost like a hierarchy of Christian service. If I'm in full-time Christian service then I'm really serving the Lord, but if you're doing an ordinary job then, 'Yeah, you're not quite there, brother.'

No. No … I think that every job can have equal value, whether you're in full-time church ministry or whatever you happen to do … We shouldn't be feeling like, because its not a full-time Christian ministry, it's not quite good enough.

Now as I look at it I realise that this job is for me something of a vocation. There are other jobs that I could do that are similar in terms of the sort of reward, but would be different and not be that vocational calling.

To me it's much more than a job. It's certainly a profession, but it's more than that, too. It's always been a calling. It's never been easy. I've always found it stressful because I was challenged with life-threatening situations through my work where I had to make many important decisions, quickly, which were of an intellectual as well as a practical nature. So it's always been a vocation, something that I've been committed to, not that I've found it easy.

Major Theme Three: the fulfilment that is gained from doing one's work

I go to work because I get a thrill out of coming up with an idea and seeing it executed in the marketplace.

People who start and found new organisations, not-for-profits or for-profit – they're all the same ... you don't turn up to work at 8.30 or work 9 to 5 and walk away from responsibility on Friday night, have a weekend, go to soccer games and turn up to church on Sunday mornings. That is your life, and that is what you do. ... I think there is a fundamental different set of needs that I've come to realise that people who found things or start things, or are in senior leadership of things, have; they have a very different view on life, very different demands. ... to be honest, we are privileged in our society to be able to do the things we want to do.

For me, work is a very soulish commitment and I've been very fortunate most of my life to dedicate my life to things that change people's lives, you know. I've sold cars and milk and things like that but I couldn't stay with it.

It's a very, very fulfilling career. … You know, we want meaning in our lives and we want to connect with real things. I get all that. Somewhere there, I think we've lost the fact that Jesus said that he would build his church. That it will be like, you know, the fruitfulness that I've seen in my life.

I love my work. I always have. I've never struggled to get out of bed to go to work. I love the challenge of work. I love the stimulation of work. I love the idea that I can make a difference.

I think fundamentally I go to work because it's something about imaging God. I always grew up with a strong sense that we are created to image God and that would mean for all of us that God would have us involved in some participatory way in his world. I'm always instructed by work being part of the 'good' creation, not part of the fall, and that God actually held up the completion of his creative work to involve man in the completion of it. So it's part of imaging God; it's part of God's ongoing work of creation. And it's part of God's redemptive work.

These were just three of six themes that emerged from my research, but they are the ones that most closely relate to the focus of this book. Having analysed all the responses of my participants, I arrived at ten summative conclusions:

1. Most participants recognised or valued their day-to-day work as Christian ministry. However, their perception was that their church leaders did not value it very highly as Christian ministry, if at all.

2. Neither the participants nor their church leaders appeared to hold sufficient theological understanding of the nature and value of human work. Furthermore, there was little evidence of any significant attempt to address the topic in the teaching programs of their churches.

3. Seen through the eyes of the participants, church leaders tended to portray – whether they really believed it or not – church-related work as spiritual work, and other work as secular. Furthermore, the participants all drew the conclusion that their church leaders generally ascribed a higher value to spiritual work than they did to secular work.

4. Participants did not generally accept the validity of spiritual–secular distinctions in regard to work and church activities. In fact, most participants rejected the distinction emphatically, while recognising that their church leaders and churches as cultures, held those distinctions tightly.

5. Churches were seen by participants to hold to a higher view of vocation insofar as it applies to ordained ministry and other specifically religious positions (such as mission work, youth work and other church-based activity) than to secular work.

6. The participants did not entirely reject their church's view on vocation, though many regarded it as flawed, and most participants held the view that their own work was worthy of being regarded as a vocation.

7. The participants held a strong view that church ought to be marked by a sense of community and close relationships, rather than being seen as a holy club where some are more honoured than others, because of the 'spiritual' work that they do.

8. The participants deeply desired to find a haven of community and friendship within their church environment, but had not generally been able to find this in their current church environments. Because, as a rule, they did not feel that their work or work-related

gifts were highly valued by their church, they were less likely to seek that community at church, gradually withdrawing their support by less frequent attendance and diminished engagement.

9. Workers – at least the kinds of workers represented in this study – may find extremely high levels of fulfilment in their work. They do not, then, come to church seeking personal fulfilment. They come seeking deep worship, accompanied by understanding and affirmation of their working lives. They often find that their church experience makes invalid assumptions about their needs, for example, that they need to be entertained, that teaching about the Christian life and experience needs to be dumbed down, or that they will not value deep, thoughtful engagement. They are often disappointed and even angry about this.

10. Churches make a mistake when they assume that, because people keep coming, they are necessarily engaged in and enjoying what is offered at church. In fact, many of my participants, who were generally well-regarded in their churches, rated their satisfaction with the nexus between their church experience and their work life as quite low. Some had even given up attending at all, while still holding a strong faith, and several had begun a process of reducing attendance and involvement. Those still attending regularly often were doing so from a sense of duty or life-habit, or for the sake of their family.

Conclusion

This short extract from my own research accords closely with the research done in many other places around the world.

Barna research in the USA, the work of some Faith–Work Institutes in the UK, research carried out in New Zealand – all have revealed similar findings.

It seems reasonable to conclude that the way that the local church relates to its members in terms of their working lives falls far short of what those workers would like it to achieve. Without better engagement, it is likely that churches will find it harder and harder to maintain the interest and participation of their congregations.

The thing that impressed me most, having conducted all these interviews, was not so much the content – I had predicted most of that. What impressed me was the deep passion my questions aroused. Sometimes that passion came out in strongly expressed answers, in tearful recollections of pain suffered because of a lack of appreciation from their churches, or in considerable anger at the failure of their pastors and leaders to appreciate what they do.

I realised as I reflected on all of these conversations that most churches can have no real idea of what is going through the minds of many of the people sitting meekly in their rows on Sunday morning as they stoically make their way through (I almost want to write 'suffer through') the service that the church leaders have planned so earnestly.

CHAPTER THREE
Mondayitis and Thank God It's Friday!

Is your work cursed?

Popular Christian writing on work

There has been an explosion of short, popular books on faith and work in the last decade or so. An online search will reveal hundreds of articles in journals and growing online resource repositories. There is much good material in some of them. But anyone who reads widely in this popular field will come away with one clear point in their head. The writers of these books and articles are in virtually unanimous agreement on one point: the notion that human work was 'cursed' by God as a consequence of the sin that Adam committed. Many people in thinking about the first sin and the alleged subsequent Fall completely miss the point that it was not Adam who sinned first, in the narrative, but Eve.

In this chapter, I will challenge this concept of work as being cursed by God and argue that its widespread adoption has wreaked untold damage on the minds of Christians across the West. A short passage in Genesis is generally the basis of this claim:

> And to the man he said, "Because you have listened to the voice of your wife, and have eaten of the tree about which I commanded you, 'You shall not eat of it,' cursed is the ground because of you; in toil you shall eat of it all the days of your life;" (Gen 3:17).

It is only a short passage, but let us hear what a big meal many authors have made of it. Some of the authors are well known and highly respected. Please take the trouble to glance down at the footnotes to read the titles of the books the quotes are taken from. The titles are sometimes very significant in terms of revealing the core intent of the author.

Os Guinness: 'Work is now partly creative and partly cursed.'[1]

Tim Keller: 'Work is not *itself* a curse, but it now lies with all other aspects of human life *under* the curse of sin. ... Part of the curse of work in a fallen world is its frequent fruitlessness.'[2]

David Miller: 'understanding work as a curse'[3] is a standard trope of Christian theology.

Tim Chester: 'Work becomes a burden ... frustrating, boring, stressful ... Endless emails, projects that go wrong, incompetent management – these are all part of working in a fallen world.'[4]

Gene Veith: 'we live in a fallen world, in which even our work is cursed'[5]; followed many pages later by an internal paradox: 'This then is the human condition: Work is a blessing; work is a curse ... Work is a virtue, but it is tainted by sin.'[6]

---

1 Os Guinness, *The Call: Finding and Fulfilling the Central Purpose of Your Life* (Nashville, TN: Word Publishing, 1998), p. 51.

2 Timothy Keller, *Every Good Endeavor: Connecting Your Work to God's Work* (New York: Dutton, 2012), pp. 89–90. It might be argued that Keller's current ecclesial practice at Redeemer Presbyterian Church, NY, is more moderate and affirmative of the goodness of work than some of his writing, but the focus of this section is merely to provide a summary of writings across the spectrum.

3 Miller, *God at Work*, p. 19.

4 Tim Chester, *Gospel-Centred Work: Becoming the Worker God Wants You to Be* (Epsom, Surrey, UK: The Good Book Company, 2013), p. 19.

5 Gene Edward Veith, Jr., *God at Work: Your Christian Vocation in All of Life* (Wheaton, IL: Crossway, 2002), p. 42.

6 Ibid., p. 63.

Colin Marshall and Tony Payne (a similar internal paradox?): 'Working is a good and fundamental part of being human in God's world ... This side of the Fall, work is cursed and frustrating ... but it remains good and worthwhile and necessary.'[7]

Darrell Cosden: 'Work is cursed and in order to survive he [i.e. Adam] will have to endure painful "sweat and toil".'[8] In later chapters he makes it clear that the curse has spread to us all: 'Since the Fall and under the conditions of the curse, our work and what it produces are ambivalent at best.'[9]

Kevin Costa asserted a direct link between the curse of work and the gospel, thus closely identifying work with sin; he even appears to claim that Jesus' redemption restores our daily working lives, in what is actually quite a startling redefinition of the gospel:

> Work became a curse. ... the ground was cursed, work became 'painful' and never-ending ... Jesus was sent to repair the fractured working relationship between us and God. He came to pay off the debt that bound work to its futility.[10]

Finally, Mark Bilton offered a similar view to most of the above, though he added a new element all of his own – something he called 'sanctified' work. Bilton started well, noting that it is not work that has been cursed, but the ground. But then he suggested that the purpose of Jesus' coming was to redeem us by removing the curse from the ground. Apparently this action results in our work becoming 'sanctified'. Presumably work done by unbelievers is not sanctified, but it remains unclear what the alternative to 'sanctified work' is:

---

7 Colin Marshall and Tony Payne, *The Trellis and the Vine* (Kingsford, NSW: Matthias Media, 2009), p. 137.

8 Darrell Cosden, *The Heavenly Good of Earthly Work* (Peabody, MA: Hendrickson, 2006), p. 95.

9 Ibid., p. 100.

10 Ken Costa, *God at Work* (London: Continuum, 2007), p. 19–20.

> The ground has been cursed as a consequence [of] sin's entry into the world ... But God sent the second Adam, Jesus, to redeem us from the curse. Work in its sanctified state is intrinsically good and deemed important by God.[11]

Clearly, this is a patchwork of ideas, demonstrating the breadth and range of the commonly held view that work, or the culture of work, is cursed – or at best, terribly damaged by Adam's sin. The authors include theology college lecturers, leaders in ministry training institutions, business leaders and even investment bankers. They are British, American and Australian.

All these views come from commonly available books in the Christian bookshops. It ought to be clear from this that I am not trying to build a straw man here that I can easily knock down. This concept of work being cursed, if not being an actual curse itself, is widespread, and it comes with some hefty reputational pedigrees.

This book seeks to argue that *the claim about work being cursed, or that all work since the Fall is mere frustrating toil, is not faithful to biblical revelation.* To compound the error of this claim, it has given rise to several other errors that arise naturally from it. Small wonder that Pinnock wrote at the end of a paper on the first chapters of Genesis:

> Evangelicals as a group have to receive low marks for their performance in this area of biblical interpretation. It is certainly not their finest hour. Many are still burdening their exegesis with presuppositions which need to be critically re-examined.[12]

---

11 Mark Bilton, *Monday Matters: Finding God in Your Workplace* (Mona Vale, NSW: Ark House, 2012), p. 11.

12 Clark H. Pinnock, "Climbing out of the Swamp: The Evangelical Struggle to Understand the Creation Texts," *Interpretation* XLIII, no. 2 (1989): pp. 152–3. Pinnock's article referred extensively to the debate around creation vs. evolution, but in the later sections, immediately preceding this quotation,

There are some writings in the popular realm that have given more nuanced and thoughtful positions than those I've quoted above, but they are not common. Larive cautiously noted: 'There is also the curse of the expulsion from Eden, often identified as the curse of having to work.'[13]

But again, the writer has gone well beyond the text. God does not announce the expulsion from Eden as a curse at all. On the contrary, it is a blessing. God does not want them to eat of the Tree of Life in this rebellious condition. What that actually means is not for discussion here, but the point I want to insist on is that when we read Genesis, we must read what is actually written, and not read our own ideas into the text.

One of the more balanced of the comments in a popular-level book comes from Hugh Whelchel, who stated clearly: 'Work is not a curse, but a gift from God ... although the Fall because of its curse made it inevitable that sometimes work would be frustrating and feel meaningless.'[14] Yet again, however, we need to ask just exactly how we might get from a Fall (which is not mentioned anywhere in the text) to work being frustrating or meaningless, 'sometimes'. Why only 'sometimes'?

Even if it could be shown that many of the writers quoted above may actually subscribe to Whelchel's slightly more balanced view – this is not what their writing commonly states, as is clear in the many examples provided above.

All of these quotations come from books published for mass audiences and written by respected, popular writers. Most of them have been sold in large numbers. If you go to

---

he included reference to the events and effects of the Fall of the first human pair, thus making his comment relevant to this study.

13 Armand Larive, *After Sunday: A Theology of Work* (New York: Continuum, 2004), p. 23.

14 Whelchel, *How Then Should We Work? Rediscovering the Biblical Doctrine of Work*, p. 13.

your local Christian bookstore, these are some of the books you will find. They are books that pastors and 'lay' people read, because they do not make time to read more serious academic or scholarly writing.

I have used here the adjective 'popular' for written/audio/visual material that is presented, largely in layperson terms, for the mass Christian market. Academic or scholarly writing, on the other hand, is generally much more moderate and carefully nuanced in its opinions. It takes into account, with careful referencing, the views of a wide range of other writers, including those who may not agree with what the particular writer is saying.

These two categories – popular and scholarly or academic – are not always easy to separate. In reality what exists is more a spectrum of writing: at one end is material clearly written for a popular audience, and at the other is that written for scholarly audiences. Some writers, e.g. Guinness, Keller and Miller, are respected academics, but they often write for popular audiences. Keller's *Every Good Endeavour* is one example.

The problem is that this sort of popular material finds its way into sermons preached by pastors who do not make time to read more serious theological texts, and who resort to these popular books for their sermon material. As a result, even those church attenders who may not read such books themselves come away with a wrong view. The casual reader or listener who attends church is most likely to absorb the idea from their respected church leaders that their day-to-day work is curse-affected.

One sermon on work, preached locally in my own city, included this statement: 'Work is a blessing, but work is also a curse. ... The original blessing is now a curse.'[15] Any lack

---

15 This principle of work as a curse as a result of the Fall was named in a series of five sermons preached at a local church on work. Stuart Cameron,

of internal logic in claims such as this tends to be lost on casual listeners in rapid sermon delivery, while the impact of the concept lives on. It may be possible to hear in this short quotation, echoes of the second reference from Gene Veith above, perhaps demonstrating the effect that popular books can have in influencing sermon preparation.

Scholarly Christian writing on work

Even scholarly writing, which is generally less inclined to be dramatic or direct, has sometimes made the claim that work suffers from being 'under a curse', or 'under the effect of a curse', if not actually cursed. It is not entirely clear what difference there is between these two concepts, anyway. Surely if a curse is pronounced on someone or something, that person or thing is now not only cursed, but also 'under' a curse and 'under the effect of' that curse!

Perhaps the mere fact that so many writers choose the softer kinds of expressions over the raw 'cursed' indicates that they are just a little uneasy about the accuracy of their argument?

Miroslav Volf, for example, declared: 'There is no suggestion in this text of work itself being a curse'.[16] Yet he asserted in the very next sentence: 'But it clearly says that, as a consequence of the curse against the ground, work has assumed the *character of toil*' (italics original). The text probably does say that about Adam's work, but it is not at all as clear in the text as Volf asserts, that all human work has assumed the character of toil.

Volf went on to use words such as 'drudgery' and 'hardship', in contrast with 'fulfilling' work prior to the curse being implemented. I intend to show below, that work-as-drudgery

---

Faith@Work: Thistles and Thorns, podcast audio, Sermon preached at Newlife Uniting Church, Gold Coast, 20 July, 2014, http://subsplash.com/newlifeuniting/v/b1523c3. At 12 mins. 45 secs. Cited 3 September, 2015.
16 Volf, *Work in the Spirit*, p. 128.

may not be as established in scripture as Volf suggested. Volf is not alone in this view, of course.

The Roman Catholic Encyclical *Laborem Exercens* declared: 'All work, whether manual or intellectual, is inevitably linked with toil. … The original blessing of work … is contrasted with the curse that sin brought with it.'[17] Those of us who enjoy our work might raise our eyebrows at this claim: 'All work … is inevitably linked with toil.'

We might also struggle with Volf's statement that work could only be fulfilling before the Fall, and that we are condemned to work-as-drudgery or toil. Certainly the participants in my research made it very clear that their work was a source of their very life. They loved it and couldn't get enough of it. None of them would have dreamed of describing their work in such derogatory terms.

If we have struggled with either of these previous two statements (Volf and John Paul II), then we are likely to spit out our morning cornflakes when we read Jurgen Moltmann: 'Not work itself, but work after the fall is regarded as work cursed by toil, pain, and uselessness.'[18]

Uselessness? Tell that to the obstetrician, to the paramedic, to the engineer, to the airline pilot, to the person who cooks your breakfast or grows your food or makes your clothes or builds your house and connects your indoor plumbing.

Nor will we be helped very much by the usually reliable Chris Wright: 'work in itself became toilsome and frustrating because of the curse on the earth. Work is no longer simply part of the joy and privilege of our human nature, but has

17 John Paul II, *Laborem Exercens (on Human Work): Encyclical Letter of the Supreme Pontiff on Human Work.* V 27. (1981)

18 Jurgen Moltmann, *On Human Dignity: Political Theology and Ethics* (Philadelphia, PA: Fortress Press, 1984), p. 40.

become a bondage and necessity.'[19]

It must be said that all of these authors are very heavy hitters in the theological world. Could they all be mistaken? Is it possible that there is another way to look at this? I have to confess to some temerity in daring to challenge these hefty scholars. But a challenge is needed. And I will not be the only one to challenge, as you will see.

Consequences of the idea of work being cursed

I have spent my life being a disturber of paradigms – and often getting into trouble for it. Given *my* nervousness at daring to disagree with such big names, I sympathise with the average church-attender who is forced to conclude that his or her work must be cursed. Their pastor has told them so. No-one wants to stand up in church and tell their pastor that he has just made a mistake in his sermon. It's easier to assume that these people who write books and give sermons for a living actually know what they're talking about.

If all our work is 'cursed', 'fruitless', 'painful', 'a bondage' or 'a tragic necessity', it is no wonder that pastors sometimes encourage young people to give up study and ordinary jobs to enter something called full-time Christian service. (We'll delve more into this in Chapter Five.)

I've always been puzzled by this, though. If all work is cursed, how is it that the work of pastors and missionaries and worship leaders and youth leaders is not? How does their work avoid the curse? But *if it were true* that it is only our *secular* work that is cursed, it is no wonder that so many university students who are keen to follow Jesus find it an easy choice to give up their study of biology or genetics or business to become

---

19 Christopher J. H. Wright, *Old Testament Ethics for the People of God* (Downers Grove, IL: InterVarsity Press, 2004), p. 151.

short-term mission workers or youth leaders.

I have not infrequently been deeply disappointed when I saw yet another of my finest school graduates persuaded by their local church to give up their important study of medicine or law a couple of years into their university course. Their family may have prepared them for this over decades, spent vast sums on fees and general living costs, just to see their son or daughter go on a short-term mission or try out as a band member or youth leader at their church. In some cases, they have never returned to their original study.

No wonder there is a general view that Monday is the most miserable day of the week. No wonder the community at large jokes about POETS Day and TGIF on Fridays.[20]

If the work-as-curse notion is not actually correct, then the church may have foisted a destructive ideology on the world that has had catastrophic effects on society. Why should atheistic communism have been the one to champion the benefits of human labour, when God appointed it unto humanity for his and our glory?

The 'work-as-curse' (or its diminutive cousins 'cursed-work' and 'work-as-burdensome-toil') principle has such a long and distinguished pedigree that it cannot be questioned without a reasonable alternative being put in its place. The remainder of this chapter will be devoted to proposing an alternative way of thinking about curse and Fall. The following chapter will build a biblical perspective of what it means to work – either as a Christian or as a non-believer.

---

20 For those not familiar with these humorous acronyms: POETS Day: *P*** off early; tomorrow's Saturday.* TGIF: *Thank God it's Friday!*

Historical perspectives on work and curse

At the time of the Reformation, Luther's and Calvin's writings on the value of human work laid the foundations for the Protestant work ethic and the revolution of respect for the work of ordinary people. Before the Reformation, religious art typically portrayed biblical or mythological scenes. Whenever a religious person was depicted, they had a large golden halo, a nimbus, behind their head to show that they were holy, not tainted by the common elements of life, such as work.

Rembrandt and a host of other Dutch and Flemish artists changed all of this. They portrayed bakers, housewives, servants and whole villages of workers engaged in dignified work. Look at any Reformation era range of art, especially from the Dutch and Flemish Masters. They showed families at meal tables, people in taverns, talking and laughing, portraits of ordinary people. This was unthinkable before the Reformation scholars demolished the theology that the only holy activities were religious ones. Roman Catholic theologians from Pope Leo XIII[21] to the present day have emphasised similar respect for the dignity of human work.

The critical passage for this debate is generally regarded to be the entire second creation account from Genesis 2:4b to 3:24. Of this passage, Walter Brueggemann wrote: 'No text in Genesis (or likely in the entire Bible) has been more used, interpreted, and misunderstood than this text. This applies to careless, popular theology as well as to the doctrine of the church.'[22]

What is puzzling about this is that alternative interpretations

---

21 Pope Leo XIII's encyclical *Rerum Novarum* (1891) set a trend that was followed and strengthened throughout the 20th century in Catholic circles, culminating in Pope John-Paul II's encyclical *Laborem Exercens* (1981).
22 Walter Brueggemann, *Genesis: Interpretation, a Biblical Commentary for Teaching and Preaching* (Atlanta, GA: John Knox, 1982), p. 41.

are not hard to find; nor are they new.[23] Scholars such as Von Rad, writing almost a half a century ago, disputed the idea that work should be regarded as cursed. Staying closely with the text, he noted that the curse is actually placed on the ground, not the man's work.

> If this curse were to have a universal effect, flowing beyond Adam, as we might assume from the general nature and genre of the whole narrative, it would be more likely to be in the form of 'an alienation that expresses itself in a silent dogged struggle between man and soil. Now it is as though a spell lay on the earth which makes her deny man the easy produce of subsistence.'[24]

Despite recognising a likelihood of toil, Von Rad maintained the scriptural insistence on the dignity of work: 'Must it be emphasised that the passage ***does not*** consider work in itself a punishment and curse? Work was ordained for man even in paradise ...'.[25] (Emphasis mine.) The German scholar, Claus Westermann was in substantial agreement with Von Rad, noting that 'work brings human life to fulfilment. ... The commission ... to work was received as, and remains a gift.'[26]

These scholars are renowned as giants of exegesis in their field of the Old Testament. Their work is well known. Anyone who seeks to comment on Genesis should at least consult them – even if they don't accept all that they wrote. How can it be that so many popular moderns have simply chosen to ignore their work? Is it really possible that they are simply ignorant of it?

---

23 See also Kenneth A. Mathews, *Genesis 1–11:26, Vol.1a*, The New American Commentary (Nashville, TN: Broadman & Holman, 2002), p. 56.
24 Gerhard von Rad, *Genesis: A Commentary (Revised Edition)* (Philadelphia, PA: The Westminster Press, 1972), p. 94.
25 Ibid., pp. 94-5.
26 Claus Westermann, *Genesis 1–11: A Commentary*, trans. John J. Scullion (London: SPCK, 1984), p. 265.

Modern perspectives on work and curse

It is time to consider another contemporary scholar. (Of course, Brueggemann should be considered a contemporary modern, too.)

Ruth Ostring, writing in 2015, acknowledged 'that "curse" in the Genesis narrative may be defined as a powerfully expressed negative pronouncement on human activity'.[27] She pointed out, however, that the Adamic ground-curse is only the first of several curses: 'God pronounces four of the primordial curses, and Noah utters the fifth.'[28] The second[29] of those curses was provoked by Cain after he had killed his brother, and affects Cain's use of the ground.

The third primordial curse identified by Ostring is implied in God's statement after the flood: *I will never again curse the ground any more because of humankind for the inclination of the human heart is evil from youth* (Gen 8:21). She infers that God regarded the flood as his latest curse on the ground.

The ground is by this stage thrice-cursed, for different reasons, and covering a much larger scope than mere work (if it ever covered that!). It is a reasonable question to ask whether part of God's promise not to curse the ground again, might allow us to infer the ground was no longer cursed by then, anyway.

In any event, to interpret this post-flood promise of God as meaning, 'Well, the ground should be thoroughly cursed now – I won't curse it any further,' would seem to be a rather curmudgeonly view of the grace of God, given that he spoke

27 Elizabeth Ostring, "The Theology of Human Work as Found in the Genesis Narrative Compared with the Co-Creationist Theology of Human Work," (Ph. D. Thesis submitted to The Faculty of Theology, Avondale College of Higher Education, NSW: http://research.avondale.edu.au/cgi/viewcontent.cgi?article=1003&context=theses_phd, 2015), p. 147.

28 Ibid., p. 148.

29 The first, of course, is found in the Genesis 3:16–19 passage.

these words in the immediate context of his gracious promise of the rainbow and a renewed blessing to fill the earth and rule over it.

The value of Ostring's work for this question is that it has highlighted the range and shades of meanings of *curse* in Genesis, given its frequency in these first chapters. It raises the question as to why, for most of the popular writers on work, the original curse is still the only one that receives any attention. It is a fair question to ask, whether too much emphasis might have been placed on the first curse, and not enough on the long narrative.

British scholar Eugene Combs has challenged the notion of God as the agent of curse, arguing that it was not actually God (YHWH Elohim is the actual name used in the text) who cursed the ground. On the basis of the use of the passive participle form of the Hebrew verb, he argued that 'the ground is *[already now]* in a condition of cursedness which may be the consequence of the man's action, not necessarily YHWH Elohim's punishment.'[30]

This idea might strike some as radical, but it is one easily accessible even by readers who are limited to the English text. Both the NIV and NRSV texts state that the ground is cursed 'because of you' (Gen 3:17). Combs made a similar claim for the cursedness of the ground after Cain's murder of his brother. 'The ground is *observed by YHWH* to be cursed, just as YHWH Elohim *observed the ground to be cursed* in relation to man' *(my italics).*[31]

We routinely make similar observations when we say things such as: *The real estate market is corrupted by greedy*

---

30 Eugene Combs, "Has YHWH Cursed the Ground? Perplexity of Interpretation in Genesis 1-5," in *Ascribe to the Lord: Biblical and Other Studies in Memory of Peter C. Craigie*, ed. Lyle Eslinger and Glen Taylor (Sheffield, UK: JSOT Press, 1988), p. 276.
31 Ibid., p. 282.

investment-buyers who own multiple houses. Or: *Marriage is in a depraved condition in the West.* Or: *Social media are the curse of modern life.*

These kinds of statements reinforce the idea that the cursed effects on the environment in which we live have been caused by our own poor behaviours, our own failures to live up to God's standards. Adam's environment was the ground on which he stood – Adam means 'earth'. His life from now on will be lived in sorrow.

In Genesis 3:17, we read: 'cursed is the ground (*ha-adamah*) because of you; in toil you shall eat of it all the days of your life.' The word translated 'toil' is in Hebrew, *otzbun*. This word generally means *grief, anguish, deep sorrow*. It is exactly the same word as is used in Genesis 3:16. In a Hebrew Interlinear Bible you can see it quite clearly: *I am increasing grief [otzbun] of you and pregnancy of you; in grief [otzb] you shall give birth.* Since Adam was being expelled from the garden and from the close presence of God, it is not surprising that both he and Eve should be told that they will live in sorrow, grief, anguish (*otzb*).

The question of the origin and the meaning of the curse ought to be a critical one, but it is not one that has been widely discussed in academic (and almost never in popular) writings. That God is generally assumed in popular literature to be the cause is revealed by just two examples from popular websites at opposite ends of the evangelical spectrum.

The first is from a strongly Reformed, academic, but evangelical site: 'And God pronounced a curse on them that we who sin like them have inherited'[32]. The second comes from what may best be described as an evangelical, fundamentalist

---

32 Jon Bloom, "Jesus Came to Reverse the Curse," http://www.desiringgod. org/articles/jesus-came-to-reverse-the-curse (The *Desiring God* site is a popular source for Reformed thinking.)

site: 'After Adam chose to rebel, eating of the one fruit God had forbidden, God punished Adam and cursed the ground.'[33]

What actually happened in regard to work as a result of what is known as 'the Fall' needs to be carefully examined. A thorough examination of 'the Fall' is beyond the scope of this book, but the actuality and meaning of a permanent, one-time 'Fall' is of major significance for this topic. [34]

Christians who accept an evolutionary approach to human origins have grappled with this notion, particularly. If Adam and Eve were not historical characters who committed a sin, then the cause of human sinfulness cannot be sheeted back to someone who was not actually an historical figure.

Regardless of one's view of human origins, however, there are still major issues to be resolved in regard to the traditional notion of the Fall. Why should someone born thousands of years after Adam bear the guilt for his sin? Indeed, the Orthodox church does not accept that theology; it is only the Western church that does. Furthermore, if Eve sinned first, why should Adam's sin be regarded as the first sin?

Suffice to note here that the term 'Fall', in the way that we use it in regard to the consequence of Adam's sin, never appears in scripture. In particular, the concept never appears in

33 Roger Patterson, "Labor: A Blessing and a Curse," https://answersingenesis. org/sin/labor-blessing-curse/ (The *Answers in Genesis* site is a popular source for evangelicals and 'recent 6-day creationist' perspectives.)

34 Many scholars, e.g. Brueggemann and Westermann are quite explicit about this: 'The narrative of Genesis 2–3 does not speak of a fall. One should avoid therefore a description that differs so much from the text and is so inaccurate and deceptive.' Westermann, *Genesis 1–11: A Commentary*, p. 276. (1984) Walton deals extensively with the topic also, in John H. Walton, *The Lost World of Adam and Eve: Genesis 2–3 and the Human Origins Debate* (Downers Grove, IL: IVP Academic, 2015), p. 153-60. A very recent text that is both provocative and helpful is: Dennis R. Venema and Scot McKnight, *Adam and the Genome: Reading Scripture after Genetic Science* (Grand Rapids, MI.: BrazosPress, 2017).

the Old Testament in any form at all. Human responsibility is alive and well right through the Jewish understanding of their own scriptures.[35]

As will become clear in the next chapter, the question of the ongoing value of work may be finally determined by whether we form our conclusions on the basis of the original blessing of God given to Adam to work – or in the subsequent events after Adam's and Eve's sin, when work is by no means the main topic of God's speech.

I have not read any writer who has carried the question of all human work being cursed on this earth through to its logical conclusion. Since Jesus was human, and worked, why was his work not also cursed? If the answer is proposed: *But Jesus did not sin*, then clearly the curse of frustration is not linked to work itself, as work, but to the sinfulness of the person performing it. The question of curse has been subtly replaced by the effects of sin on human work.

That would change everything, and would raise a whole new slew of questions about whether non-believers could ever perform good work and whether Christians who are renewed in Christ, are permanently exempt from the alleged curse. Curiously, the question of the effect of sin on work might be closer to the truth than might at first appear. But that would be to go further than we intend to go just now. That is the subject of the next chapter.

---

[35] The Pseudepigrapha book, 2 Esdras 3:21-22, (4 Ezra) may offer some support: *For the first Adam, burdened with an evil heart, transgressed and was overcome, as were also all who were descended from him. Thus the disease became permanent; the law was in the people's heart along with the evil root, but what was good departed, and the evil remained.* This is not regarded (by Protestants at least) as inspired Scripture, but it may give some idea of 'what was in the air' when it was written. Scholars place its authorship between 70-218 BC. It may well have affected Augustine's writing which became definitive on this topic.

The curse on work – or the ground?

Adam's work in the narrative up to this point has not been limited to farming or gardening. He has been engaged in intellectual work, classifying and naming the creatures God had made. Reading this story on its own terms, in its own genre, forces us to recognise that work is much more than ancient agrarianism.

The tasks given to the man and woman were not a burden – they were given as the first blessing which outlined their work. The blessing-command was given to both male and female without distinction in the first creation story:

> *So God created humankind in his image, in the image of God he created them; male and female he created them. God blessed them and God said to them, 'Be fruitful and multiply, and fill the earth, and subdue it; and have dominion over the fish of the sea and over the birds of the air and over every living thing that moves upon the earth'* (Gen 1:27–8).

The man and the woman were given tasks of administration, management, family life, and development of a culture.

The most basic analysis of the core text about a curse – an analysis not requiring any expertise in ancient languages – would show that a curse was not placed on the notion of work at all. It was placed on the ground: *cursed is the ground because of you* (Gen 3:17). The negative effects of thorns and thistles, and the effort required to produce a good crop are related to the ground-curse, not to the process or concept of work.

None of the intellectual, managerial work that Adam and Eve both had presumably been doing should have come under this supposed curse on work. Furthermore, since Eve was a recipient of the blessing of work in the first creation narrative as noted above, why should her work not be under the curse of the ground that was specifically directed towards Adam? She had her own set of consequences.

Again, to follow the point through logically, if only ground-related activities were to be cursed, then it would have made much more sense for Cain to have followed his brother Abel and become a grazier. Indeed, any of the other tasks listed in Genesis 4 – metallurgy, music-making, and so on – might have been exempt from the curse.

Only a tiny percentage of people in the modern Western world work with the ground. Most of our work is done analytically, digitally, with people and services inside air-conditioned buildings, far away from mucky soil. Would a cursed ground worry us much now anyway?

The more one examines the text logically, the more one starts to see that the claims about all work being cursed are an interpretation of a divine pronouncement that wasn't discussing work anyway, and are drawing on very long bows. It is a massive step to take from hearing that Adam's garden would produce thistles to having a crowded email inbox (see the claim from Tim Chester above). It seems a huge over-reach to claim that human work will be permanently and unavoidably frustrating, toilsome, painful, useless and a bondage – all terms we have read from commentators above.

Joy to the world

In the words of one of the most beautiful Christmas carols:

No more let sins and sorrows grow
Nor thorns infest the ground
He comes to make His blessings flow
Far as the curse is found, far as the curse is found
Far as, far as the curse is found

We can see the same idea in these words as we have been hearing in this chapter. But as we think a little more deeply about it, we realise that it is an Advent carol. Jesus is born – be joyful. Why? Because he is coming into a world where there is the effect of a curse on humanity and the physical world itself. This Jesus will make his blessings flow wherever that curse is found.

We surely cannot sing this without thinking immediately about the very last chapter of the book of Revelation:

> *Then the angel showed me the river of the water of life, bright as crystal, flowing from the throne of God and of the Lamb through the middle of the street of the city. On either side of the river is the tree of life, with its twelve kinds of fruit, producing its fruit each month; and the leaves of the tree are for the healing of the nations.* **Nothing accursed will be found there any more.** *But the throne of God and of the Lamb will be in it, and his servants will worship him; they will see his face, and his name will be on their foreheads. (Rev 22:1–4)*

What do we make of this? Were all the cursed-work writers correct after all? Let's do what we should always do with scripture and let the context help us out. Context is everything.

The scene being described is the new Jerusalem, heaven come down to earth. The Tree of Life is there, so we know that we are in a setting that harks back to Genesis. Humanity was expelled from Eden because of a mortal risk:

> Then the LORD God said, "See, the man has become like one of us, knowing good and evil; and now, he might reach out his hand and take also from the tree of life, and eat, and live forever" — Therefore the LORD God sent him forth from the garden of Eden, to till the ground from which he was taken. He drove out the man; and at the east of the garden of Eden he placed the cherubim, and a sword flaming and turning to guard the way to the tree of life (Gen 3:22–24).

The problem that made it imperative to keep humankind away from the Tree of Life where they might live for ever, was that they now knew both good and evil. God can 'know' evil without risk of corruption because he is pure; he is totally and completely good; he is Original Good. Evil doesn't actually exist by itself; it is only good gone bad, good corrupted, good turned in on itself, like fruit left to rot in a bowl.[36]

But the created humans have not only *encountered* evil; they (both he and she) have *enacted* evil. Humanity (because Adam and Eve are surely symbolic representatives here) has enacted evil in the form of rebellion against God's word. They have chosen self-assertion rather than obedience to the divine Word.

They must not be allowed to live forever in this state. The Tree of Life is mortal poison to a sinful being.[37] But neither must they be allowed to die in this state, so they must be expelled, and a new human must come and live and die for them. This is the gospel promise.

It is this gospel promise that is being fulfilled in the Revelation reading above. The Lamb has conquered. The Messiah (Christ) has taken his throne. Heaven has come down to earth. Jerusalem has been redeemed. The curse is gone. Which curse? The curse of being separated from the Tree of Life. The curse of having to live in the place where you could actually die in your sins.

The absence of curse is the same as the healing of the nations. Our greatest problem is not the fact that we die. Our greatest problem is that we might die burdened with our sin and in the midst of brokenness all around us because of sin. That was a problem that only God could address, once Adam and Eve had sinned. But thanks be to God, the Messiah did come, the powers of evil were defeated, and you and I will have access to the Tree of Life in the new heavens and the new earth.

---

36 Compare: C. S. Lewis, *Mere Christianity* (New York: Macmillan, 1952), p. 46.
37 Compare 1 Cor 11:27–30. This is a passage rarely heard in many churches. I can't help but wonder if there may be a link between the prohibition that God puts in place in Genesis and Paul's teaching.

The curse has nothing to do with work. The expulsion from Eden is about separating the holy ground from the cursed ground that Adam has profaned in his sin. Work is not even remotely in view here, when we read the text properly.

Summary

It does not seem too much to ask that ministers and church leaders should be sufficiently well-versed both in academic reading and the capacity for scriptural exegesis to ensure that they focus on the positive aspects of work in their teaching. Their knowledge should not be limited by this quite massive roadblock of seeing work as a curse.

What they have failed to take sufficient notice of was shown to us by Westermann, who drew our attention to it in his commentary on Genesis. There is a cycle running through the first 11 chapters of blessings followed by curses, exiles and punitive consequences, followed again by blessings and new starts. This blessing–curse–blessing cycle repeated throughout the first 11 chapters of Genesis is a far stronger element of the story than the one single curse in the third chapter. It is also a pattern repeated throughout the entire Old Testament.

In this chapter, we have established that an emphasis on human work as being under an ongoing curse, as is strongly portrayed in popular writings and even in some academic writing, is not sustainable as a concept. Popular writings commonly try to describe work as cursed by God, or made burdensome by a curse, while also simultaneously insisting on its many positive elements, which leads to nonsensical inconsistencies.

We have established that there is a significant body of writing that has argued that the curse language of Genesis is irrelevant to the question of human work in general. On the contrary, we have hinted that, due to its divine appointment, work has inherent potential for dignity and nobility. More will be said of this in the next chapter.

Much is made of the importance of the third chapter of Genesis, especially Genesis 3:14–19, in most popular and some scholarly writing, in regard to its providing the foundations for our understanding of present human work. This is unfortunate. Overemphasis on one element of the entire creation narrative has produced an imbalance of emphasis on that one element.

There is at least a strong case to be made to downplay the rhetoric about the effects of an alleged divine curse on, or directly affecting, human work. If this case can be sustained, then both the theological understanding and the actual practice of speaking and thinking about work in the church can be reconfigured in ways that may be of great benefit.

It is widely agreed that there were several curses: that it was the ground that was cursed in at least two cases, not work itself, nor the people involved. There is reasonable doubt about whether the curse was imposed by God or whether its source is not clearly revealed to us at all. Even if it were imposed by God, there is no indication that this was done with the intention of permanently distorting human work.

In summary, it must be said that the meaning and the effect of what is popularly known as 'the curse' is anything but clear. On balance, it may be wiser to avoid making any statements about a curse at all in the context of work.

There is more than enough biblical description of work, the world at large and the sinfulness of human beings to provide us with an understanding of work in human culture, without resorting to doubtful interpretations of an event (i.e. God's response to Adam's sin) that was never intended to address the issue of work at all, at least not in a primary fashion.

In our next chapter, we will look at what the Bible writers actually have to say about the meaning and purpose of human work.

CHAPTER FOUR
Is there a Biblical View of Work?

> ***Letters patent*** *(always in the plural) are a type of legal instrument in the form of a published written order issued by a monarch, president, or other head of state, generally granting an office, right, monopoly, title, or status to a person or corporation ... Letters patent are issued for the appointment of representatives of the Crown, such as governors and governors-general of Commonwealth realms, as well as appointing a Royal Commission.*
>
> https://en.wikipedia.org/wiki/Letters_patent

In imago Dei

By this stage in our thinking about work, we might be inclined to be very sceptical of Leland Ryken's blithe statement: 'Defining work is relatively simple.'[1] Providing a simple but sufficiently profound definition of the concept of work, within biblical frameworks, is turning out to be a very complex task.[2]

Jurgen Moltmann asserted that one cannot 'arrive at a biblical doctrine of work by means of the concordance method'.[3] This view was apparently supported by Miroslav Volf – probably the most respected international expert in Faith and

---

1 Leland Ryken, *Work and Leisure in Christian Perspective* (Eugene, OR: Wipf and Stock Publishers, 1987), p. 28.

2 Preece, *The Viability of the Vocation Tradition*, p. 7.

3 Moltmann, *On Human Dignity: Political Theology and Ethics*, p. 43.

Work studies.[4] Such dismissive claims surely deserve testing, however, regardless of the stature of those making the claims.

Richard Langer, Professor of Biblical Studies and Theology at Biola University, provided the hefty kind of support that we need to encourage us as we proceed with our own critique:

> Volf rejects as naïve the notion that an adequate theology of work can be built on induction from biblical passages, but there must be a middle ground between such a simplistic theology by concordance and an authentic biblical theology.[5]

Of course, simple proof-texting would always be an inadequate foundation, but as Langer suggests, 'an authentic biblical theology' on such a significant topic may be built on firm ground, beyond naïve verse-hunting. This chapter will attempt to locate that firm ground.

We will proceed by laying down a series of seven propositions, which we will carefully support from scripture. To build a complete and thorough theology of work from scripture, we would need to range across the whole of scripture. Nevertheless, I am going to limit my argument in this chapter, predominantly to just the first 11 chapters of Genesis. I am doing this for four reasons:

1. The greatest confusion on this topic has come from what I believe to be a misinterpretation of the early chapters of Genesis.

2. To treat the whole of scripture would require a much larger book than this.

3. Genesis provides the essential building blocks on which

---

4 Volf, *Work in the Spirit*, p. 77.

5 Richard Langer, "Niggle's Leaf and Holland's Opus: Reflections on the Theological Significance of Work," *Evangelical Review of Theology* 33, no. 2 (2009): p. 108.

the rest of scripture relies for thinking about work.
Genesis is the foundation; all the rest is commentary.

4. We will examine, in Chapter Six, the effect on work that the advent and work of the Lord Jesus Christ has had.

The first 11 chapters of Genesis express a unity of thought about the nature of our world and the dynamic of our relationship with God – and his with us. (I add this last phrase, because it is a category mistake to think that we can just think about our relationship with God as we might a relationship with any other human. In human relationships, there is a kind of mutuality possible, because of our equality of being. It is not so with God.)

As a full narrative, these chapters are sometimes called, as a useful shorthand, the 'creation saga'.[6] Naturally, most people, scholars and ordinary Bible-readers alike, generally approach these chapters for other reasons than to think about work. The saga is rich in information about many topics: origins in general, ontologies (who we are as humans and who God is), sin, salvation-history, cosmology, just to name a few.

Proposition #1: The whole of the first 11 chapters of Genesis forms a better basis for thinking about work than just a few verses in one chapter.

Christians and the church in general have suffered from reading this creation saga too often as a series of single, individual stories: the first seven days, the paradise garden, the expulsion from Eden, the narrative of Cain and Abel, the flood, the tower, and so on. These sub-narratives easily fit into a Sunday School curriculum, lectionary readings, or a series of sermons. Each one takes about the amount of time to read that

---

6 See M. C. Steenberg, *Irenaeus on Creation: The Cosmic Christ and the Saga of Redemption* (Leiden, Netherlands: Brill, 2008).

a person might typically spend on a daily reading. As a result, we have neglected to read them as a whole, and have missed one of the most important points about them.

Each of the single stories has stand-alone integrity, but in addition they fit around or over or into the others, rather like Russian dolls. Each gives further insight into the whole, as it is fitted over the previous story. Taking a satellite view of the whole structure can help us by acting as a corrective, warning us against majoring too much on the minors of a single element.

When we need to, we can take out one of the 'dolls' and play with it for a while; but we must remember to put it back in its place and keep the whole thing together. Recognising this layered, progressive structure will discourage us from focusing too much on single sentences or individual events. We will be thus discouraged from using such singular moments as major planks for theological arguments.

Thinking about the different stories in this 'Russian doll' mode helps us to make sense of things that otherwise might appear to be inconsistent. A serious inconsistency, or worse, several of them, might lead some to abandon their faith in the entire book. No doubt this has happened to many church-goers who have become spooked by the apparent inconsistencies. When external commentators, such as Richard Dawkins or other public critics of the Bible, approach the text in this cherry-picking mode, we cannot insist on their treating the text with the integrity due to it if we have not done so ourselves.

For example, in the first creation story, God appears to make the man and woman together, more or less simultaneously and with no sense of hierarchy. In the second story, however, the narrator describes a different process, quite separated by time and purpose and function. In the second story, the woman is derived from the man, and her making is thus separate from his. The two stories are fundamentally different.

Clearly both cannot be true in an identical literal sense. The Russian doll model helps us to read them as two ways of telling a story about humanity and about God. The first story may be more about God, and the second more about humanity. The one story-doll fits inside the other. There are other apparent conflicts in the saga that will be helped by thinking about them in this mode.

Questions such as where Cain found a wife, or how he managed to found a city, when the narrative has only indicated a mere handful of people on the earth – if it were taken as a literalist account – start to make more sense when we stop reading it as a simple linear history. Taking the long view might help us to think about why the saga commences with God's creative word resounding throughout the heavens, and ends with humanity's confused words at the Tower of Babel after they had (perhaps) sought to conquer heaven.

The first time we stand back and view the full landscape of the creation saga, it may hit us with something of a shock to find that *work inhabits almost every page.* Work is not just the domain of Adam in the garden, yet this is almost the only work domain that most popular books on the topic consider.

The whole narrative starts with God working; and then God stands back while humans take over. Farming, animal husbandry, home-making, construction, various technologies, music-making, boat-making, viticulture, architecture, exploration …

Some of the work receives divine disapproval. Some is a response to divine directives. Mostly, however, it is descriptive of what people do, often as a minor element, incidental to other matters. Occasionally it is portrayed as a deliberate action of obedience to or rebellion against God's word-and-will. There is a series of consequences/ blessings/ curses in response to how people live and what they do.

Of course, there is a lot more happening in these 11 chapters – humans making choices for or against righteousness, development of family life, emerging concepts of sin and forgiveness, and more. Nevertheless, reading the story of humankind in the first 11 chapters of Genesis as the story of *Homo laborans* (human-the-worker) is a reasonable response. People work; that is what we do.

Much of the human work is in response to a divine instruction that arrived in the form of a blessing (Gen 1:28), and was repeated at least once (Gen 9:1–7). Other elements of the work are in apparent rebellion against God. The notion of a curse on work, *as work* – or even work that is deeply flawed by a curse on the environment – is notably absent. At no point does the narrator ever suggest that the work that is being done is destined for frustration, nor that it is seen as miserable toil.

No doubt it was with just this kind of observation in mind, that Combs noted 'a quiet but consistent teaching of the text about … the human propensity to bias transmission with the view that God is responsible, not man, for those harsh conditions associated with death'.[7] Careful and faithful readers who are committed to the inspiration of scripture will nonetheless recognise that untruths are sometimes placed into the mouths of characters within that scripture. The devil's words in the temptation of Jesus narrative are just one example of many.

Human work is an inherent element of the narrative, right across the entire 11 chapters of the creation saga, even if it is not specifically mentioned in every story. The saga as a whole, and in its various parts, operates as scripture to pattern and to question our lives, to clarify who we are, and thus to inform our thinking about work.

---

[7] Combs, "Has YHWH Cursed the Ground? Perplexity of Interpretation in Genesis 1-5," p. 286.

Proposition #2: Human work at its best mirrors God's work: order-making, organising, ruling – work that is fruitful, productive and good.

Throughout the 11 chapters of this saga, we see the basic human need 'to create order, to establish categories, to differentiate like from unlike – in short to impose a patina of orderliness on the essential untidiness of our existence'.[8]

This order-making is a pattern we see right from the first creation account, in which God-the-Worker imposes order on the chaos of *tohu va bohu*, the *formlessness and emptiness*, in the second verse of the first chapter. It is the Spirit of God who energises and organises the chaotic space, working, until the performative word is spoken, *Let there be light!*

It is this conversion from formlessness to order that Susan Niditch termed *the first transformative type of work*, the movement from chaos to cosmos.[9] It becomes a formative model for much human work, creative, technical and theoretical. God's work was ordering, converting and ruling, and it is this same sort of work that was given by God to humanity (both male and female) in Genesis 1:26–8.

It is as though God demonstrates what work is, then says, 'Now you do it!' This role-modelling prepares the way for human work as ordering and ruling done *in the place of* God, i.e. as God's viceroys. This concept will form the substance of Proposition #4.

The movement towards order is constituted in the text by word and deed. First, God speaks, then he acts. The spoken words are performative in themselves, but God is also active in deed. We, as humans *in imago Dei*, learn from God that our work is both intellectual and manual, and respond accordingly.

---

8 Susan Niditch, *Chaos to Cosmos: Studies in Biblical Patterns of Creation* (Chico, CA: Scholars Press, 1985), p. 6.

9 Ibid., 6.

We image or mirror his work.

We bless. We nurture. We speak performative words: *You are now husband and wife ... Her name shall be Talia. ... I baptise you ... This bread is the body of our Lord Jesus Christ.* We build; we make; we create.

Much of the work in the saga (or, for that matter, in our own human lives) does not look in the least as though it were suffering under a curse. Our marriage-making and children-making is often joyful, noble and God-honouring, as is our building, inventing, healing, farming, and nurturing of animal life. There is every reason to suppose, in the absence of any textual information to the contrary, that it was similar for those described in the saga.

Clearly a simple curse-consciousness does not fit the total reality. The glum pronouncements on 'work as toil' that we have read above, do not match the reality of life as many of us know it now, and as the characters in the saga knew it then. Our work is better than that. For many of us, we enjoy our work, even if it wearies us. There is little to suggest that all the technological advances of music-making, ironmongery, construction[10] and so on were frustrating toil, burdensome and tiring – and they were certainly not *useless*.

The fact that some of the technologies were used for weaponry or for other rebellious purposes does not spoil the argument. The technologies themselves were the divinely intended consequences of stewardship of the earth and its resources. A refined metal can be crafted by human hands into either a sword or a ploughshare. How men and women used the technologies was a matter of obedience or rebellion; the technologies themselves were neither moral nor immoral. It is no different for the human beings and technologies of today.

It actually looks in the saga as though people were enjoying

---

10 See Genesis 4:19–22.

themselves, albeit within the normal ups and downs of human life – and the constant negative consequences of sinful human actions. Reading the whole saga and taking a long view helps us to 'see'[11] our own work, the patterns of our own lives, more truly.

Of course, this is not our experience of all human work over all time, in all places. Many humans throughout history have found work to be difficult and burdensome. It is still so for many in the present age. We do not need to deny that fact in order to argue this case. We will address this problem under the next Proposition.

Ancient societies tended to regard celebrations and rest from work as high points of community life – but celebrations of the *completion* of work do not necessarily imply that the work was despised or not enjoyed. Indeed, our own celebration of a completed project often says a great deal about the enjoyment gained from working on that project.

It beggars the imagination to think that for thousands of years of agriculture, manufacture, hunting or gathering, it would not have been part of the human condition for communities, at particular times, to enjoy and exult in their healthful and productive work – a successful hunt, completion of planting, end of harvest, building of a house, birth of children, weddings, and other celebrations. In fact, community celebrations were commonly centred around work-related events such as harvests and first-fruits.

Most of the classical (i.e. Roman and Greek) literature available to us that belittles work comes from the lordly classes. They no doubt enjoyed the benefits of servants and serfs. They could extol the benefit of idleness because they were

---

11 By using 'see', here, I mean to echo the 'and God saw' refrain in the first chapter. In our seeing (examining, evaluating, stepping back to admire) of our work, we echo this divine pattern, too.

rich or powerful enough to have others to do their work. It was the wealthy Greeks and Romans with slaves and servants who wrote disparagingly of work, but never actually did any themselves.

However, we also have extensive records of people in that age enjoying and appreciating work. Their literature and artwork are replete with examples of people enjoying planting, harvesting and wine-treading. Artistic inscriptions on Greek and other ancient pottery show scenes of workers celebrating such events and activities.

The situation becomes even clearer away from curse-oriented Western influences. Various ancient Asian poets extol the joy of life and work; consider just one example from T'ao Ch'ien, a Chinese poet:

> *Ploughing is done*
> *   and also I have sown ...*
> *Contentedly I sit*
> *   and pour the new spring wine,*
> *Or go out to pluck*
> *   vegetables in my garden ...* [12]

From the Hebrew world, many midrashim contain praises to work. Here is one such:

> There is merit and even dignity in handicraft. Do not say, 'I need not work for my living, but cast my hope on God who supports all living creatures.' You must work for a livelihood and look up to God to bless the work of your hands. Jacob, in alluding to the delivery from Laban's house, says, 'God hath seen the labour of my hands.' [13]

All of these examples demonstrate that work has not always

---

[12] T'ao Ch'ien, "On Reading the Classic of the Hills and Seas" in Cyril Birch, ed. *Anthology of Chinese Literature*, vol. I (Harmondsworth, Middlesex, UK: Penguin, 1965), p. 203.

[13] "Midrash Tanhuma," http://www.sacred-texts.com/jud/midrash.htm.

been viewed as toil and drudgery. The evidence from history, literature and the arts supports the claim that work has not always been miserable, frustrating toil, despite what some modern Western writers have claimed.

We can look both in the creation saga and in the rest of scripture for reasons for the less enjoyable experiences of work. Inevitably, human sinfulness will underpin whatever reasons are found. Exploitation of the underprivileged, war, selfishness, carelessness for human dignity, lack of respect for gender, class, age, ethnicity – all of these will form part of the explanations for work as toil.

What must be stressed, if we are to give a biblically faithful account of work, is that sinful human actions are highly likely to turn work into laborious toil. Greed, exploitation, violence – these are just a few of our human habits which can turn the blessing and privilege of work into toil.

There is nothing in the nature of work, as work, however, that makes it inherently cursed or a curse. If work is toil, if it is dehumanising, if it is boring, the fault is ours, not God's. How dare we, like Lamech, blame God for what we have done to ruin his good plans (Gen 5:29).

But this has already taken us into our Third Proposition …

Proposition #3: The human work described in the saga is an extended parable about all human work: the point is not that work is cursed, but that human rebellion is the reality that too often diminishes or even destroys the ideal.

The ideal of the first two chapters of Genesis does not last long; it soon descends to the harsh realities that we recognise in our daily working lives.[14] A careful reading of the whole saga will reveal reasons for this tragic descent.

This movement through the creation saga, from the harmony

---

14 Niditch, *Chaos to Cosmos: Studies in Biblical Patterns of Creation,* p. 6.

of life in the garden to the reality of broken relationships, lost hopes, spoiled potential, estrangement from God, family stress, squandered resources – these portray life as it has been known for millennia. In the 11 chapters of the saga, we meet the same elements repeatedly, often in increasing degree and with escalating consequences, including murder, wholesale destruction, revenge, and community rebellion against God.

Over and over again, in the saga we repeatedly see God responding to this rebellion. Let us be clear about this: it is rebellion that is at the heart of the poor choices throughout the saga, not a curse on work. God clearly tells Cain that he has a choice to make:

> The LORD said to Cain, 'Why are you angry, and why has your countenance fallen? If you do well, will you not be accepted? And if you do not do well, sin is lurking at the door; its desire is for you, but you must master it' (Gen 4:6–7).

There would be no point in God telling Cain to grow up and make some personal choices, take some personal responsibility if, indeed, the curse (or a Fall) had made it impossible for him to do so. Likewise, God seems to suggest that those who might think about killing Cain will have to bear the responsibility of their choices: 'Whoever kills Cain will suffer a sevenfold vengeance' (Gen 4:15).

The whole point of the flood story was that the entire human race had been acting rebelliously – as a matter of choice. In the story, God sent a flood both as punishment and renewal: not renewal of human character – but renewal of opportunity. The characters that emerge from the ark are still the same as they were when they entered the ark. The earth is still the same except that now it has been cursed three times – once after Adam, once after Cain, and now with the flood.

Then the saga honestly and starkly records that this new

opportunity barely lasted five minutes, historically speaking. Noah lay in his tent, naked and in a drunken stupor. His son, Ham, somehow offended his father – it is not entirely clear how – and yet another curse is declared. This time, it is Noah who does the cursing. The curse falls, oddly perhaps, not on Ham, but on his son, Canaan.

When it comes to the story of the Tower of Babel, we see the same pattern. Immediately after the flood: *God blessed Noah and his sons, and said to them, 'Be fruitful and multiply, and fill the earth.'* (Gen 9:1) God has repeated his command to be fruitful and fill the earth. The inhabitants of Babel reject this word of God to be prolific and expansive upon the earth, and instead choose to build the tower. Note carefully their reason: *let us make a name for ourselves; otherwise we shall be scattered abroad upon the face of the whole earth.* (Gen 11:4)

The same pattern seems to be repeated time and again throughout the entire saga. God gives a word to be obeyed. Humankind, either individually or in community, disobeys and rebels, going its own way. God (or one of the human characters in the narrative) responds in punishment or pronouncement of some consequence.

There are occasional new starts (the birth of Cain as the first child, the birth of Seth, the life of Noah, the post-flood beginning, and so on), but the hoped-for ideal always gets muddied into a same-old, same-old reality. It is in these transformations that we learn who God is, how he relates to us, who we are, how we should and should not live with one another and with God, and how God transforms us.

This is why I called the entire saga an extended parable of human work and life. It tells a story – or better, a series of stories – that is symptomatic of the pattern of humankind over history, and of God's responses to our obedience or rebellion.

Perhaps the greatest human degradation of work is the practice of slavery or hostile indenture of labour. There is no clear reference to slavery in the saga, though it quietly occupies the background throughout much of scripture. That is to be expected; scriptural writers told the stories of their era. Slavery was part of their story.

Slavery is perhaps the lowest point to which we humans can sink in regards to our working selves. Scripture never gives approval to it, and we can easily work out from first principles, as we have learned already in the saga, that slavery is not the kind of work that God has envisaged for humankind.

The essence of slavery is the improper use of human resources. The creation mandate to live *in imago Dei*, stewarding the earth's resources, was repeated after the flood to Noah – but with the added requirement for proper respect for both human and animal life (Gen 9:1–7).[15]

Work done under conditions of slavery is the result of the slave-owner's rebellion against this mandate, and always lacks human dignity. It is false logic to thereby condemn work as a curse, when the fault is clearly of human origin, not of work itself.

The point that is being stressed in this proposition is that work is not *by definition* suffering from cursedness. It is often enjoyable and fulfilling. Sometimes our environment or our fellows make our work into 'frustrating toil' to be sure, but it is also often bright and creative, often transformative, often refreshing. 'The reality presented is not all inherently evil or depressing. It is reality – and indeed this reality is dynamic with birth and death, growth and decline.'[16]

The frustrations do not seem to be the result of an inherent

---

15 For a thoughtful analysis of this, see Brueggemann, *Teaching and Preaching*, p. 83. (1982)

16 Niditch, *Chaos to Cosmos: Studies in Biblical Patterns of Creation*, p. 37.

cursed nature of work as work, so much as the actions of sinful human beings, and their misuse of the structures and technologies they have developed. We recall, however, that even God's work of creation was frustrated by human sin. And here we must again be brutally logical. If we can argue backwards from our current work frustration to a cause of human sin, how do we explain the fact that God's work of creation was also frustrated? Surely he did not sin?

So we reach a conclusion: Work in itself is not cursed, but it is inevitably performed by, and among, people who are inclined to act in sinful ways. These sinful responses sometimes spoil the joy of work. In fact, work remains God's blessing to us, and is one of the principal means by which God intends us to cooperatively complete the transformation of chaos into kingdom.[17]

Blessing and curse/judgement form a frequently repeated motif throughout the 11 chapters of the creation saga, and indeed the whole of the Old Testament.

Proposition #4: Human work involves ruling the entire creation on behalf of God.

We have now arrived at the very heart and core of the key to a biblical understanding of work. You may like to check the definition of this book's title in the box at the head of this chapter, before reading on.

Standing at the beginning of this complex narrative, is one outstandingly significant element.[18] In the first act of creation

---

17 As Barnes says, 'Such an understanding of work, however, is contrary to the historic teachings of the church, which has, over the years, emphasised the "work as curse" mentality.' Kenneth J. A. Barnes, "A Theology of Work for a Post-Industrial Workplace," http://marketplaceinstitute.org/2013/02/papers-httpmarketplaceinstitute-files-wordpress-com201302a-theology-of-work-for-a-post-industrial-workplace-pdf/.

18 Earlier, we critiqued the popular focus on curse on the grounds that it was

of humankind, God declared the male *and* female beings to be rulers:

> *Then God said, 'Let us make humankind in our image, according to our likeness; and let them **have dominion [rule]** over the fish of the sea, and over the birds of the air, and over the cattle, and over all the wild animals of the earth, and over every creeping thing that creeps upon the earth.' So God created **humankind** in his image, in the image of God he created them; **male and female he created them**. God blessed them and God said to them, 'Be fruitful and multiply, and fill the earth, and subdue it; and **have dominion [rule]** over the fish of the sea and over the birds of the air and over every living thing that moves upon the earth'* (Gen 1:26–8).

The word used for *dominion* or *rule* is not one that implies force or abuse of power.[19] Rather, humans are to take their place as image-bearers of the High King. When the ancient writer of this narrative put these words together, he was writing into a culture that understood what it was for a god's image to be physically placed somewhere in a community.

In the ancient world, a wood or stone image was commonly deployed as a *de facto* presence of the god.[20] It meant that

---

based on a single passage that had no clear reference to work. We suggested that to rely on one passage for such a major plank was inadequate. It might be argued that here, we are doing the same thing. This is not so, for two important reasons. (a) This passage clearly is relevant to human work. It describes work in close detail in three different forms. The connection to work is clear and undeniable. (b) The instruction-blessing as we are calling it does not appear once only. It is repeated after the flood, in 9:1–7. This repetition is significant because it is made to the new post-flood world, in much the same terms as it was to the first new world.

19 Victor P. Hamilton, *The Book of Genesis: Chapters 1-17* (Grand Rapids, MI: William B. Eerdmans, 1990), p. 139. Also in Westermann, *Genesis 1–11: A Commentary*, p. 161.

20 Peter Enns, *The Evolution of Adam: What the Bible Does and Doesn't Say About Human Origins* (Grand Rapids, MI: Brazos Press, 2012), p. 139.

this community, this land, this space, this field, this building, wherever the image was placed, was under the control and administration of that god. Gerhard von Rad wrote in his commentary on Genesis:

> Just as powerful earthly kings, to indicate their claim to dominion, erect an image of themselves in the provinces of their empire where they do not personally appear, so man is placed upon earth in God's image as God's sovereign emblem.[21]

Farmers in predominantly Catholic Bavaria place little covered 'tabernacles' for statues of Mary or Jesus or the Holy Family in their fields, even to this day, to claim their blessing over the produce of the land.

In the ancient world, humans were most often regarded as servants, playthings or nuisances by the mythical gods. Their gods lusted after the beautiful women; they hated powerful men; they fought with one another, in 'titanic' struggles, using human beings as pawns. Very often, their creation narratives told of how the gods created humankind to serve the gods and make their lives easier. Read any of the ancient mythologies – you will find that this is the common pattern for interactions between gods and humanity. As Shakespeare wrote, in *King Lear*: *As flies to wanton boys are we to the gods; they kill us for their sport.*

This Genesis narrative was like a meteor flash appearing in the mental skyscape of the ancient world. This Creator God, *YHWH Elohim*, did not use humankind as his toy, nor selfishly as his despised servant. He actually made distinctively-gendered men and women in his very own image, and placed them in the world to govern it with real authority and real responsibility.

Human beings – note well, this meant men and women

---

21 von Rad, *Genesis: A Commentary (Revised Edition)*, p. 60.

from the very beginning – rule the world *as if God were ruling it*. We rule it in his stead. It is as if God placed us on this planet and then withdrew to heaven, leaving us to it.[22] It is important that we note the stress on both men and women.

The very modern angst about the lack of regard for the work of women cannot be sheeted home to a patriarchal religion, despite what ignorant television panellists claim. It is yet another example of how work has been dehumanised by human rebellion and disobedience. In its origins, work was equally to be performed by male and female, with no distinction.

The *imago Dei* (image of God) principle[23] of Genesis acts in precisely the same way as an imperial power sets up a colony or vassal kingdom: 'the human species is installed as God's vice-regent [sic] over all creation with power to control it and regulate it, to harness its clear potential.'[24] The word 'vice-regent' here is actually a misuse. This is an important distinction. The correct term is 'viceroy'. The Oxford Dictionary's definition of 'viceroy' reads: *A ruler exercising authority in a colony on behalf of a sovereign.*[25]

A *viceroy* acts for a monarch *who is not present in that place*, e.g. a colony in a distant land, such as Australia or India or Canada, under the Royal Throne of England. A *vice-regent* acts

---

22 I stress that clearly God has not actually gone away and left his creation. The concept of ruling *in imago Dei* depends on what lawyers sometimes call a legal fiction. God has not left us abandoned; but we act, and he wants us to act, *as if* he were not here.

23 The definitive text on *Imago Dei* is: J. Richard Middleton, *The Liberating Image: The Imago Dei in Genesis 1* (Grand Rapids, MI: Brazos, 2005). Any investigation of this topic that does not consult Middleton is really only paddling in the shallows. For his detailed examination of humanity's royal agency, see especially pp213–9.

24 William J. Dumbrell, *The Search for Order: Biblical Eschatology in Focus* (Eugene, OR: Wipf and Stock, 2001), p. 20.

25 Oxford Dictionaries, (Oxford University, 2016), http://www.oxforddictionaries.com/definition/english/viceroy. Cited 5 September, 2016.

as a deputy for a monarch who is actually present in that place. The expressions are commonly confused, even in Australia where we ought to know better. Our Head of State is the Governor-General, who is sometimes (incorrectly) described as a vice-regent, rather than (correctly) a vice-regal person or a viceroy.

God's 'absence' in this creation narrative is demonstrated by expressions such as 'Let us go down …' in Genesis 11:5–7, and in the preamble to the flood narrative. While God is, of course, always present in some form – his omnipresence is one of his undeniable attributes – the point of the humans acting *in imago Dei* is that God has, *in practical effect*, withdrawn, leaving humankind to act in his place. It is our job now to run this place. That is the clear message of Genesis 1:26–30.

This concept is of enormous and foundational significance to our developing concept of work, illuminating what it is that people are actually doing in their day-to-day work. *Imago Dei* work tasks are not all grand, spiritual, impressive tasks; they are the ordinary stuff from which the everyday life of any human community is made.

To claim that God has cursed our work is to utterly degrade the most foundational concept of creation: humankind (male and female) made in the image of God, doing the work that God would do if he were 'here'. It should now be clear why I have been so insistent in my rejection of that claim.

Whether our work is manual, technical or theoretical, and regardless of who performs it, it will reflect some aspect of, and response to, the blessing-to-rule (1:28). This has relevance for later discussions of vocation and the contemporary confusion in churches over what might comprise secular work and spiritual work.

Proposition #5: *All work, when done with a profound consciousness of acting 'in imago Dei', always honours God, always seeks to act in obedience to his word-and-will.*

We may need to be reminded of the meaning of the word *obedience*. It is not a popular word in this independent and rebellious age. Our word *obedience* comes from the Latin *audire*, to *hear*. When we obey someone's instruction, we *hear* it and *do* it. The Hebrew word for *obey* comes from the same root as *hear*, in Hebrew, exactly as we have in English, from the Latin. To obey is first to hear, and then to act on what is heard.

Throughout the entire saga, work is seen as the natural human response to the word-and-will of God, even if this 'word-and-will' is sometimes ignored or debased. I will be using these as a singular noun, *word-and-will*, hereafter, to stress the inseparability of the two concepts. The word-and-will of God is present always and in all places. It is how people respond to that word-and-will, either with or without intentional, obedient faithfulness, resulting in either harmony or conflict, holiness or rebellion.

The saga introduces us to a way of thinking about the world that is distinctively God-responsive. This responsiveness is very different from mere obedience to a command. The pagan gods demanded obedience in ways that were arbitrary and sometimes vengeful. YHWH Elohim's word-and-will always requires a human response that emerges from relationship. God's word-and-will is more commonly mediated via covenant, rather than commandment.

The response will be either *obedience* or *rebellion*. When the response is *rebellion*, the human agent, by rejecting the proffered relationship, is acting on their own self-serving, self-worshipping authority. When it is *obedience*, the response comes from the properly worshipful recognition of the creature-to-Creator relationship that is in place. As Brueggemann says: 'It is a way in which obedience is known to be the mode of the world willed by God. But this is not obedience which is required or demanded. It is a grateful obedience embodied as doxology.'[26]

Do you see the sheer beauty of this? Our daily work-as-obedience forms and shapes our praise and worship. This is true whether we are stacking supermarket shelves, performing life-saving surgery, preaching a sermon or cooking a meal for the family dinner.

Understanding this concept provides the critical corrective to the mistaken 'work-as-curse' theology. It is not that human work is inherently cursed – it is potentially doing the very work of God, but human choices may render it rebellious anti-service. This concept of rebellious work will form the content of Proposition #6.

Obedience-as-worship is equally open to all who work. It is not especially offered only to those who do 'religious' work. Cain did not pause to wonder if his sacrifice had been rejected because his younger brother might have been called to ordination with divine approval to officiate at the altar, while he was 'only' a farmer. The story focuses rather on heart and motive – the choice to praise through the work of obedience (or the obedience of work, which derives from the former) or to honour only self.

Sin 'is lurking at the door' (Gen 4:6–7), but there was a free choice for Cain as to how he dealt with it. Otherwise, God's warning to him was cruel and pointless. Human beings are free to decide about their own work-futures, their own allegiances and whom they worship.[27] This freedom is glorious

---

26 Brueggemann, *Teaching and Preaching*, p. 14. (1982)

27 'Human work has an ethical value of its own, which clearly and directly remains linked to the fact that the one who carries it out is a person, a

but dangerous.

Thus N. T. Wright described the link between worship and work as the 'covenant of vocation'.[28] When this covenant is broken, by our refusal to work within God's boundaries, by our failure to act as responsible stewards (or images), it is a 'vocational failure as much as ... a moral failure'.[29] Failure to work well is a failure to worship well; it betrays our fundamental human purpose.

Old Testament work is never far from praise and worship, though sometimes, in rebellion and rejection of Yahweh, choosing idolatry rather than obedience: '*Avodah* is the transliteration of the Hebrew word for both *worship* and *work*. The root word means to work or to serve ... Work involves the idea of serving someone.'[30]

In the New Testament, Jesus told us to pray that God's kingdom might come. If we understand work well, we see that *our work performs that enacted prayer as we seek to do God's work with him, building his kingdom on earth and in heaven.* If we see our work in this way, we will refuse to see it as mere frustration and burdensome toil.

Work that is performed in keeping with our status as beings *in imago Dei* is never far from our service to, cooperation with, and worship of God.

Barnes commented that 'Such a "high view" of work must be at the centre of one's theology of work, if that theology is going

---

conscious and free subject, that is to say a subject that decides about himself.' John Paul II, *Laborem Exercens (on Human Work): Encyclical Letter of the Supreme Pontiff on Human Work*. II:6.

28 Tom Wright, *The Day the Revolution Began* (London: SPCK, 2016), p. 102.
29 Ibid., p. 103.
30 William D. Bjoraker, "Word Study: (Avodah) - Work/Worship," (2016), http://ag.org/top/church_workers/wrshp_gen_avodah.cfm. Cited 26 August, 2016.

to foster positive attitudes and constructive relationships.'[31] Unfortunately, as he explained, this high view of work has not been traditionally found in the life of the church, especially not in modern times.

Proposition 6: Work done in disobedience or rebellion may still be called work, but it is not work according to the model of work mandated in Genesis for humankind.

Many years ago, I was sitting with a group of school principals chatting about our schools. A colleague was telling a story about a young man who had been caught spray-painting graffiti on his school buildings. The damage was extensive and costly to repair. The police had brought the young offender up to the school to meet the principal and apologise for his actions.

In the course of the meeting, the young man said something like: 'I've painted graffiti all over my suburb. It's what I do! It's not rubbish. It's art. You should come and see some of my work on the water tower!'

My colleague spat back at the young man, indignation massing in his voice as he replied, 'Work! Work! You call that work?!? That's not work! That's vandalism! Work is about doing something useful!'

Who was right – the young graffiti vandal or the principal? Is this a binary option, or is there room for more than one truth in a world of relativism? Is one person's work another person's destruction? This question demands an answer.

Human beings are always active. They do things that take effort. There is much human activity that looks like work, but is actually destructive and disobedient, e.g. warmongering, crime, vandalism, and destructive or exploitative activities of any kind. Effort expended in such life-destructive activity,

---

31 Barnes, "A Theology of Work" p. 7.

done against the word-and-will of God, is not work – at least not in terms of the definition we are using in this text.

This disobedient, rebellious activity is a kind of anti-work. It brings no blessing, and serves only false idols. We have already made the point that work and worship are almost identical words in Hebrew. Anti-work is worship of false gods, e.g. self, money, power, fame, bravado, and so on.

Remember our three categories of human work (from Genesis 3:26–8): fruitfulness, subduing, and ruling or having dominion. Human activity that is not life-affirming (replenishing, *fruitful*), sustainably *subduing*, nor *ruling* in vice-regal dominion – is not truly work in the biblical sense – it is rebellion against the purpose of humankind as set by God. It will look like work, and often be called work, but that's only because we don't have another name for it.

Such rebellious activity might include kinds of apparent *fruitfulness* that are not actually affirming of human life. These could include some kinds of cloning that remove individuation; IVF practices that select particular lives (while destroying others as surplus, or unsatisfactory for some reason); or engineered life designed to suit selfish or discriminatory ends, such as gender-preference, or appearance- or ability-based selection. It might include growing crops (tobacco, for example) or synthesising illegal drugs that are harmful to the humans who consume them.

Other rebellious activity might include *subduing* practices that are destructive of sustainable ecosystems, involve damaging or exploitative genetic manipulation, or which cause the exploitation or harm of local inhabitants or workers.

They might also include *ruling* that is violent or destructive of life (e.g. warfare) or human culture (annexation of regions, ethnic cleansing, capitalistic or cultural imperialisms, and the like); political control that diminishes human dignity or creates (or protects) injustice; or commercial management practices that deny human flourishing and dignity.

This kind of human activity, which looks like work but is destructive and rebellious towards God, may be described as *bent*. Luther famously taught that sin changed our nature to be *incurvatus in se*, bent in on itself.[32] C. S. Lewis used the concept of a 'bent world' throughout his science fiction trilogy, to describe the character of a sinful world from the perspective of inhabitants of other planets. Such a world needs repairing.[33]

The understanding of work that we are developing here resolves a difficulty that others have observed: how to define or describe human activity that is destructive or illegal and yet appears not structurally different from good work. This acknowledged difficulty has not generally been satisfactorily dealt with.

Miroslav Volf claimed that 'all human work is done in the power of the Spirit'.[34] This is surely a difficult claim to substantiate. What about Stalin's murderous work? The hard physical work of managing the daily business of Auschwitz? The work of terrorists? The work of criminals in planning and executing a complex robbery or fraud scheme? The work of computer hackers and scammers who prey on vulnerable users online?

Following the thread we have pursued so far, we can say that the destructive 'work' of war, of crime, of political or civic activity that denies human flourishing, of rapacious activity

---

32 David S. Yeago, "The Catholic Luther," *First Things* Vol. 61, March (1996): p. 40.

33 Hence the Jewish concept of *tikkun olam* – repairing the world. For a finae exposition of this concept, read Jonathan Sacks, *To Heal a Fractured World: The Ethics of Responsibility* (London: Continuum, 2005).

34 Volf seems to ignore the 'work' of criminals, earth-destroyers, exploiters of the poor, or warmongers, in suggesting that 'all human work is done *in the power of the Spirit'*. Volf, *Work in the Spirit*, p. 118.

against the earth, its resources or its people, is not truly work in its divine purpose.

It is activity, to be sure; it may look deceptively like work, but it is futile, rebellious activity (un-work) directed against the word-and-will of God. Any work (whether performed by Christian or non-believer) that does not meet the life-affirming, subduing, obedient character of work (see Proposition #5) falls into the category of rebellious activity.

The ancients had a word for the kind of negativity that drove the young graffiti vandal to whom I referred above. The word was *acedia*, one of the seven deadly sins. We probably prefer to use the word 'sloth'. Sloth is not mere laziness, as it is commonly used. The ancient vice of acedia/sloth was vastly different from mere laziness. Sloth sets in when a person has so far given up on the quest for, or the love of Truth, Beauty and Goodness, that they resort to damage, defacing or destruction of anything that shows those characteristics.

Thus vandals destroy private or public gardens, ripping up plants in wanton destruction. Thus people spray graffiti on public or private property, seeking out new blank surfaces that they can deface. Thus comedians, rap artists or actors mouth the foulest curses and swearwords that they can, just so that they can sully things that are, or were once, lovely. Thus artists create destructive social statements such as the deliberately provocative installation known as 'Piss Christ'.[35] The final outcome of sloth is the death of meaning. It ultimately ends in suicide and the death of culture.

It is not sufficient – and there is no sound biblical ground

---

35 This 'artwork' is a photograph of a crucifix immersed in a vat of the artist's urine. Similar 'works' include such items as Piero Manzini's 'Artist's Shit' – a collection of 90 sealed cans filled with the artist's own faeces; or Chris Ofili's 'Holy Virgin Mary' – a collage of pornographic cut-outs and elephant dung.

– to assume that God will somehow divinely re-order this 'anti-work' for good purposes.[36] It must be named for what it is, destruction rather than production, rebellion rather than obedience.[37] This is the point of the multiple curses throughout Genesis 1–11 that we met earlier. Understanding and teaching this distinction is essential for church leaders in guiding their congregations in how to think well about their work.

Understanding this is vital for parents and teachers to help young people learn how to manage their world of study, work, and preparation for adulthood.

Proposition 7: *The story that unites the creation saga with the rest of scripture, and ultimately the Gospel narrative, is the story of the uniting of the man and the woman.*

The inclusion of the nuptial relationship of man and woman – the two different genders are theologically important – may not seem at first glance to be related to the topic of work. In fact, it is very closely related.

The creation saga, in which male and female humans were given tasks to do as in the image of God, to manage the world of animals and plants, is *the* foundational passage of scripture with respect to the relationship between the two genders. Jesus believed it to be so, as is clear from his reference to it

---

36 This ultimate, blanket blessing on all the work of non-believers is how I read Volf, 117–9. (Volf allows himself a caveat at the end of this section, but the caveat does not sufficiently mitigate the foregoing assumption of blessing: 'To the extent that non-Christians are open to the prompting of the Spirit…' p. 119.)

37 It is precisely this 'anti-work' that comes under the judgement of God in Revelation 18; the work of the beast that came out of the earth (13:11–18), and whose number was 666, is all of that activity that looks like work but which is directed towards the glory of man rather than God. It is described in detail in that chapter, but perhaps especially in 18:21–23.

when he was asked about marriage.[38] We should expect to see within this passage, then, some hint of the gospel, of the grand redemption narrative. The gospel narrative is not unconnected with the topic of work.

Try reading the narrative this way:

There is a planet that is the focus of attention of the Most High God. You might call him *El Elyon*.[39] In a tremendous act of creative power, he had brought that planet into existence a very long time ago. In doing so, he also created an entire cosmos, with stars, planets and suns – all in a vast and expanding universe.

All of the rest of the universe outside the planet on which he has placed his favour are not our concern just now. The planet we call Earth is the focus of this grand narrative.

The Most High God prepares this planet, endows it with life and the potential to grow and nurture life. He creates a particular form of life, called Man and Woman – Humans, Beings. These creatures, unlike all other created beings on this planet, possess moral agency — the capacity to choose to act morally, i.e. for right or wrong, good or evil.

To these creatures, he grants his Royal Permission to manage the entire planet, including all of its creatures and resources, on his behalf. The only requirement is that the man and the woman hear and obey God's word, worshipping God alone. Their glory is in their nuptial commitment of love to each other, as they join their hands in work and service to their Creator.

When the woman sins by choosing words other than God's words, the man accepts her guilt, entering into it as his guilt, and together they come under the judgement of God. Now,

---

38 Mt 19:3–6.

39 This name for God is one which sets him apart from all the other claimants to Deity in the ancient world. Every pagan tribe had its gods, but both Melchizedek's and Abraham's God was *God Most High*. See Gen. 14:18–22. The text calls God: *El Elyon*, God Most High, Creator of heaven and earth.

being separated from the holy, close and deep relationship with God that they had both known, they are forced to manage their lives in their own strength.

God does not remove from them their Great Commission. Indeed, after a great and terrible judgement, he renews it. They are still to be his hands and his feet and his voice in the world – but now they are not to live in the close and holy relationship with the Most High God that they once enjoyed. They are re-commissioned, however, to take the word of God to the world, and to rule and manage it.

The man and woman, throughout their generations, rebel and fail to do their task well. At the end of the creation saga, which tells their story in the microcosm of their descendants' lives, there is widespread rebellion and failure. The human race is dispersed and disunited.

God still does not remove his Great Commission, but now, in the chapters immediately following the saga, he renews it with a new man, Abraham, and his wife, Sarah. Their story becomes the story of Israel, the nation tasked with giving the words of God to the world. Israel's glory is in its *marriage* to God's words and their *faithfulness* to the word-and-will of God. This story eventually also folds into faithlessness and rebellion.

Finally, the Most High God who created the universe takes the sin of the world into himself, entering into the world, taking on its guilt and placing himself under his own judgement. This Most High God chooses to do this by becoming a man himself, while still remaining God in the mystery of his Trinitarian Being.

Through this deep mystery of truly sacrificial love, the Most High God is able to redeem his created people and his created universe. His promise is that he will return to renew the entire creation in glory and righteousness. At that time, he will 'wed' himself to his 'bride', the church. Together, we, the church, with our God, will work in perfect cooperation to manage the kingdom of God. This new age will be ushered in with a Great Wedding Banquet in the heavenly halls.

It is this vision of nuptial bliss that the prophet Hosea envisioned (Hos 2:16–23):

> *On that day, says the LORD, you will call me, "My husband," and no longer will you call me, "My Baal." For I will remove the names of the Baals from her mouth, and they shall be mentioned by name no more. I will make for you a covenant on that day with the wild animals, the birds of the air, and the creeping things of the ground; and I will abolish the bow, the sword, and war from the land; and I will make you lie down in safety. And I will take you for my wife forever; I will take you for my wife in righteousness and in justice, in steadfast love, and in mercy. I will take you for my wife in faithfulness; and you shall know the LORD.*
>
> *On that day I will answer, says the LORD, I will answer the heavens and they shall answer the earth; and the earth shall answer the grain, the wine, and the oil, and they shall answer Jezreel; and I will sow him for myself in the land.*
>
> *And I will have pity on Lo-ruhamah, and I will say to Lo-ammi, "You are my people"; and he shall say, "You are my God."*

The day-to-day work that we do, even now, is linked to this exciting redemption narrative. The story incorporates the joy of an earth that is fruitful and responsive to nurturing hands. Our work, pre-figuring this final work of God, forms a part of the greatest love story ever told. God has worked, first to create the world, then to redeem it and us, and he calls us to work with him to see that redemption complete.

As if this were not enough, there is still a further element to this Proposition. I have been referring above to the Great Commission that was given to Adam and Eve. I used that expression with a particular intent. Most of us will be familiar with the Great Commission – as we call it – in Matthew 28:18–20.

> *Jesus came and said to them, "All authority in heaven and on earth has been given to me. Go therefore and make disciples of all nations, baptizing them in the name of the Father and of the Son and of the Holy Spirit, and teaching them to obey everything that I have commanded you. And remember, I am with you always, to the end of the age."*

We might notice a strong similarity between this commission and the one that God gave to those who started a new world in the Genesis narrative – Adam and Eve, and Noah.

Jesus declares that he holds authority, because he has been given it by God. That was understood of God in the first Genesis chapter, simply because of his Creatorship. Then Jesus grants to the disciples tasks of **fruitfulness**: *go and make disciples*; of **subduing**: *baptising them*; and of **ruling**: *teaching them to obey*.

The Bridegroom is taking his authority and giving his Bride, the church, the tasks she needs to perform while he is 'absent'. But this absence will be just like the one in Genesis. He won't really be absent, even though he is not 'here'. As he says: '*I am with you always.*'

The voice of the prophets

There is a sort of inverse argument to be made about the question of work-as-curse from the various prophetic books of the Old Testament. I will only treat it briefly here, but it is an important perspective to hold in our minds. The argument forms a codicil to the seven propositions above.

The Old Testament prophets routinely castigated Israel and Judah for a range of faults in their social practice. Some of their fierce denunciations were directed towards false religious practices, where the Israelites had abandoned their God and gone over to the worship of idols and false gods.

That kind of prophetic utterance is relevant to our topic, because of the close relationship between work and worship, as we discussed in Proposition #5 above. However, the other focus of their denunciations is even more relevant.

The prophets also frequently denounced the people of God for poor work practices. The use of dishonest scales, fraudulent commercial practice, violent social life, the exploitation of the poor and of widows by taking their land or treating them oppressively – all these raised the ire of most of the prophets.

This voice is perhaps strongest in some of the minor prophets, but it is there also in the words of Isaiah, Jeremiah and Ezekiel. Consider just a few examples from many that could be listed:

> *For I know how many are your transgressions,*
> *and how great are your sins—*
> *you who afflict the righteous, who take a bribe,*
> *and push aside the needy in the gate.*
> *Therefore the prudent will keep silent in such a time;*
> *for it is an evil time.* (Amos 5:12–13)

> *Alas for those who devise wickedness*
> *and evil deeds on their beds!*
> *When the morning dawns, they perform it,*
> *because it is in their power.*
> *They covet fields, and seize them;*
> *houses, and take them away;*
> *they oppress householder and house,*
> *people and their inheritance.* (Micah 2:1–2)

> *The LORD enters into judgment*
> *with the elders and princes of his people:*

> *"It is you who have devoured the vineyard;*
> *the spoil of the poor is in your houses.*
> *What do you mean by crushing my people,*
> *by grinding the face of the poor?" says the* LORD GOD *of*
> *hosts* (Is. 3:14–15).

Abraham Joshua Heschel wrote about the role of the prophets:

> The prophet is a man who feels fiercely. God has thrust a
> burden upon his soul and he is bowed and stunned at
> man's fierce greed. ... Prophecy is the voice that God has
> lent to the silent agony, a voice to the plundered poor, to
> the profaned riches of the world. ... God is raging in the
> prophet's words.[40]

For the purpose of this book, we might ask: why is there such
a 'silent agony'? Why would God be 'raging' because some
widows were defrauded, some poor people exploited? Surely
their idolatry and worship of false gods were worse than some
mere economic or social failures?

The answer lies in the fact that, as we have seen above, God
has required men and women to manage the world *as God
would if he were 'here'*. When we imaged beings fail to do that,
we actually tell lies about God. We blaspheme his holiness. Our
exploitation looks to the world as though we were saying, *This
is how God acts.*

The book of the minor prophet, Habakkuk is essentially a
meditation on two frequently repeated ideas in the Hebrew
Bible: the principles of *kiddush ha-Shem* and *chillul ha-Shem*.[41]
These refer, respectively, to the sanctification (*kiddush*) and the
desecration (*chillul*) of God's Name.

The foundation for this principle is in Leviticus 22:31–32.

---

40 Abraham Joshua Heschel, *The Prophets*, vol. 1 (New York: Harper &
Row, 1969), p. 5.
41 For an extended discussion of this concept, see: Sacks, *To Heal a Fractured
World: The Ethics of Responsibility*, pp. 57–70.

Thus you shall keep my commandments and observe them. I am the LORD. You shall not profane my holy name, that I may be sanctified among the people of Israel.

The Holiness of God is an essential concept in Jewish life. It is the very foundation of the Law. More than that, it is the heart of who God is. The prophets repeatedly talk about how Israel had profaned God's name:

They sell the righteous for silver, and the needy for a pair of sandals;

They who trample the head of the poor into the dust of the earth, and push the afflicted out of the way; father and son go in to the same girl, so that my holy name is profaned; (Amos 2:6–8)

Here, the prophet Amos condemns exploitation of the poor and sexual immorality as *chillul ha-Shem* – the profaning of the holy name. Here is the essential point. *When human beings who are called to act in imago Dei, who are called to act as viceroys in the place of God himself, behave badly or act immorally and unjustly, we profane the name of God.*

If none of the other arguments about work not being a curse convince us, surely this one should! When we work honourably, acting genuinely as though we were God himself acting in the world, our work sanctifies or honours the name of God. Could anything be further from a curse? When we act badly, below the standards of holiness that we should operate on, we profane God's name, God's reputation. It is not that our work has been cursed by God. On the contrary, our work can either be a sanctification or a desecration of God's holy name.

The prophets held a divinely inspired, high view of all men and women as the image-bearers of the Most High God – and thus the infinite value and exquisite preciousness of all human beings in God's eyes. When, through our disobedience to God's commands, our work demeans that preciousness, that infinite value of human beings in the face of God, we effectively make God look evil.

Creation, work, curse – a summary

We have covered a vast amount of ground here. A short summary is in order.

The creation narratives in the first 11 chapters of Genesis must be read as a whole. Although the saga commences with a blessing from God, which is reiterated more than once, there is also a series of curses. This blessing/curse/blessing is the story of the human race in microcosm. The sustained sense is not so much a single moment of Fall as a constant rebellion. Human beings are rebels who must lay down their arms.[42]

These first 11 chapters set out the problem of humankind: our sin, our rebellion, our worship of false gods. The rest of the Bible, starting immediately with Abraham who was to be a blessing to the nations, is the solution to the problem so carefully laid out in the creation saga.

The essential human metanarrative – our big story – is that as human beings, we are made in the image of God, to rule over the entire creation as stewards, filling the earth with family and working to create shalom and achieve justice, acting in obedient response to the word-and-will of God.

Our task orientation in this stewardship role ought to be that of benevolent, careful and caring rulers, acting on behalf of the Creator-King:

> The biblical view of dominion … is one of sacrificial service. The Old Testament model of rulership is that of a benevolent king who rescues the oppressed and has compassion on the needy, weak, and afflicted (Ps 72:2–4, 12–14).[43]

---

42 Lewis, *Mere Christianity*, p. 56. (1952)
43 Keith B. Miller, "Theological Implications of an Evolving Creation,"

Despite this noble goal, the narrative demonstrates the utter impossibility of humankind ever achieving righteous obedience in purely human strength of will. It seems clear from scripture that human beings have an inherent disposition to sin,[44] but it is also apparent that we have agency and capacity to obey God's word, if we choose that way.

It is undeniable that throughout the entire Old Testament, including the various parts of the creation saga, human beings are offered choices.[45] A prime example is in Deuteronomy 27:9—28:68, where obedience is clearly outlined and expected; and again in Deuteronomy 30:11–15, where 'following God's commands is presented as simply a matter of choosing what is easily accessible'[46]:

> *Surely this commandment that I am commanding you today is not too hard for you, nor is it too far away ... No, the word is very near to you; it is in your mouth and in your heart for you to observe. See, I have set before you today life and prosperity, death and adversity.*

Work in all of the creation narratives describes the real-world activities of human beings as they respond in daily life to the need for survival, and to the word-and-will of God in managing and subduing the creation, sometimes well, sometimes in rebellious activity.

At its best, human work is akin to worship, serving God in obedience and humility, creating shalom and nurturing life. At its worst, it is destructive of life and actively works against the word-and-will of God. In this 'mixture of faithful obedience and recalcitrant self-assertion ... the negative response tends

---

Perspectives on Science and Christian Faith 45, no. 3 (1993): pp. 158–9.

44 See, e.g. Genesis 8:21; Psalm 51:5; Job 14:1–4; Romans 3:12 – but there are many other similar passages.

45 Enns, *The Evolution of Adam: What the Bible Does and Doesn't Say About Human Origins*, p. 87.

46 Ibid.

to dominate the narrative.[47]

The glory of the humans in this creation narrative is that they are God's chosen creatures to help him restore the creation, destroy evil and establish God's kingdom not only on earth but in all the heavens as well.

A thoughtful reading of the Genesis narrative will conclude that work is not cursed by God, nor made into burdensome toil in consequence of the sin of Adam. Work is a divine gift, that resonates with the character of the male–female being that God made, *Homo laborans*. It is a gift because human-the-worker is made in the image of God-the-Worker. The capacity to manage our environment, changing it, developing it, nurturing it, as individuals and in families, is a gift of God, mirroring God's own work of creation.

The human environment in which we work is inclined towards rebellion, for reasons we are not clearly told. All rebellion ultimately consists of recognising neither God-the-Creator nor our responsibility as created beings to serve and worship that God. A more accurate phrase than 'inherited sin' is 'inherent tendency to sin', and this is consistent with the entire Old Testament text.

When we work well, we honour God's name. When we do poor work, or act immorally, we desecrate God's name. We do our work with a constant choice before us. Will we act as though we were God, doing justly, loving mercy and living in humility? Or will we act in contradiction to the holy name of God?

Paul makes it clear that people are not merely ignorant of God. He asserts that they are very aware of who God is, but that they deliberately suppress that awareness, *as a matter of deliberate choice*, and persuade themselves to believe, or to claim that they believe a lie:

---

47 Brueggemann, *Teaching and Preaching*, p. 13. (1982)

> *For the wrath of God is revealed from heaven against all ungodliness and wickedness of those who by their wickedness suppress the truth. For what can be known about God is plain to them, because God has shown it to them. Ever since the creation of the world his eternal power and divine nature, invisible though they are, have been understood and seen through the things he has made. So they are without excuse* (Rom 1:18–20).

Our human environment frequently immerses us in widespread human rebellion. This ensures that our work is often frustrated and made difficult, or even intolerable, by the actions of sinful people (including ourselves), *but not by any inherent quality of work being subject to a curse.*

Nevertheless, those who follow Jesus Christ as Creator-King continue to work and worship, as servants and stewards of God, in sure and certain hope of the coming final redemption to be fulfilled on the basis of that which has already been achieved on the cross. Thus Tolkien wrote, recognising the fulfilment of the ancient narrative in the work of Christ:

> The Christian has still to work, with mind as well as body, to suffer, hope, and die; but he may now perceive that all his bents and faculties have a purpose, which can be redeemed ... All tales may come true; and yet, at the last, [be] redeemed.[48]

This redemption is the eucatastrophe,[49] the joy that was promised from the beginning. This is as it should be, for the giver is all joy in very character.

---

48 Christopher Tolkien, ed. *J. R. R. Tolkien: The Monsters and the Critics and Other Essays* (London: HarperCollins, 1983), p. 156–7.

49 Tolkien's special word for the joy of the solution of the human dilemma found only in Jesus Christ. *I coined the word 'eucatastrophe': the sudden happy turn in a story which pierces you with a joy that brings tears.* Letter 89, Tolkien Gateway Wiki, "Eucatastrophe," http://tolkiengateway.net/wiki/Eucatastrophe.

A glimpse of this joy is found in the relation of man and woman in the early part of this creation story. It is deeply true in its resolution of the break that sundered the former relationship of the man with the woman, and of the humans with God. It will be deeply true again, when those relationships are restored in the marriage of the King and his Bride, living and working together in the restored heaven and earth.

The pronouncements that God makes after the man's and woman's sin has been uncovered are not so much punishments as covenantal declarations. It is as though this loving God is saying, *This is the way things will be from now on. They are not all as they were, but you may look to the future with joy, even though your way will be much harder now than it was to be before you disobeyed me.*

She shall deeply desire him, and he shall work with the cursed ground, and their desire and their work shall form the basis, not only of their marriage, but also of their children and family. Their relationship will image the grand story of the coming joy of the Marriage of Christ and his Bride. In fact, it will do much more than merely image it. The humans will live out this redemption story in their new life upon and for this material earth. This work-within-relationship will sacramentalise their new life. It will express in its wholeness the mystery (Greek *mysterium* = Latin *sacrament*) and glory of the coming joy.[50]

It is not only love and marriage that tells the story of redemption; it is work – work that deals with forms and materials and environments that do not grow truly or reflect truly the realities and goodness of beautiful truth. As workers

---

50 For a fuller analysis of this concept, outlined in Proposition #7 above, and summarised here, see: Ephraim Radner, *Hope among the Fragments: The Broken Church and Its Engagement of Scripture* (Grand Rapids, MI: Brazos Press, 2004), pp. 121-38.

we bend, shape, re-create, and even invent new forms, new tools and new ways of dealing with the world that will, like Niggle's leaf, finally be fully redeemed.[51]

The value of our work's production is not only in its promise of future kingdom realities. Our work holds value in the ever-present, truth-in-living realities now, in the drawing together of ourselves with others in our lives and our communities, and in the integration of our own mind, heart and spirit. Far from being a curse or burdensome toil, our work is the sacramental marker of our calling as viceroys, and the enacted hope of our redemption, the coming eucatastrophe.

The ancient Hebrew celebrating the first-fruits was no less looking forward to the joy of redemption than is the child carrying her basket of ripe fruits to the altar rail in the Harvest Festival. Likewise, the electrician, the CEO or the volunteer carer must be taught to recognise their work-purpose to partner in Christ's restoring of the cursed ground to the good earth,[52] which will ultimately be married to the good heaven.

This is the task of the Bride of Christ, the church.

---

51 *Leaf by Niggle*, a short story about work and human life, available in J. R. R. Tolkien, "Leaf by Niggle," in *The Tolkien Reader* (New York: Ballantine, 1978).

52 Pss 80:9; 85:1–11; 65:9–11.

CHAPTER FIVE
What Is God Calling Me to Do?

The notion of calling or vocation

My personal experience

Although this book attempts to go well beyond the narrow sense of vocation as a calling to ordained ministry, it would not be complete without some reference to it. My own story may be relevant as an introduction.

I have been involved in church activities from as early as I can remember, and I have reflected on the issue of 'full-time Christian service' and what it means to be 'called into ministry' for over forty years.

In my early years, I seriously considered entering an ordained ministry profession. I re-visited the possibility often, as I heard impassioned pleas from pulpits and in personal conversations to become a minister or missionary of one kind or another, forsaking my ordinary daily work for what was termed 'full-time Christian ministry'.

As I considered this possible vocation, I tried to understand why ordination meant different things to different churches. If this were truly a divine call, how was it that different Christian organisations set down such widely different pathways?

The paths to ordination varied in acceptance requirements, length of study, and in the privileges of what tasks could be performed once ordained. Even the titles ultimately conferred (such as Reverend, Father or Pastor) seemed to mean quite varied roles. In one church, you even had to remain unmarried.

At the most informal end of the spectrum, one could become an ordained or credentialed minister with very little theological qualification – certainly no tertiary degree required. Meanwhile, any member in good standing in those churches could preach, teach and preside over ceremonies of baptism, the Lord's Supper, and funerals without any training whatsoever.[1] Indeed, in the low 'Brethren Assembly' type of churches, no ministers were credentialed at all.

In other churches at the more formal end of the spectrum, the requirements were quite demanding: three to five years of tertiary study, plus at least one year as a deacon or acolyte of some sort. Those members of the congregation who were not ordained or specially licensed were not permitted to do much more than attend, and perform some simple rostered tasks such as welcoming and reading set scriptures or prayers.

These quite different expectations and practices, not to mention the absence of any common view of the distinctions between 'lay' and 'ordained' in the wider Christian church, drew into question for me the very relevance of those categories. Who was to say what was 'right', in the apparent absence of any clear scriptural basis?

In that era, at least in my circles, churches reserved ordination for men only. Women were excluded from ordination. Even as a child, I wondered at the large number of women missionaries who came to speak at my church. They all told stories of churches they were leading in foreign lands such as Africa or Papua New Guinea, even though none of them would have been allowed to become a minister among us white folk in an 'advanced' country. I remember, as quite a young

---

1 This was, and still is the case in most Pentecostal churches, as well as the 'low' denominations such as Apostolic or Full Gospel (Brethren). Baptist churches were sometimes similarly open though they required a more formal period of training for ordination.

child, asking my father about this apparent paradox.

In my late 20s, I was strongly encouraged by my church to leave my job and study to become an ordained minister. This period of discernment was a weighty time for me, and, not insignificantly, my wife. Part of the final decision not to take this step was my (our) conclusion that I could serve God just as well in my daily work as I could in ordained ministry.

Any divine call, if one were to exist at all, I concluded, was more likely to be a call to service, faithfulness and discipleship, rather than to a particular, formal role. I did not have a well-devised theology or biblical justification for this – it was more of a hunch. It would take me years to work out the biblical basis for this opinion.

That decision has defined my life as a worker. Whatever 'day-job' I had, I was always strongly involved in my local church, preaching and assisting in various roles, as permitted by the various denominations I have attended. I learned to submit to the 'club rules' of the various churches to which I belonged.

Some churches require particular preparation for ordination, and have different rules of engagement for those who are ordained than for those who are not. I simply concluded that I needed to submit to these rules as a part of my agreement to be a member at that church. I did not need to agree with them in every sense, to give full mental assent to them, but I should respect them.

That is simply a human duty, in the same way that a member of a golf club must respect the club rules. It is also a Christian duty to respect the authorities of those in positions of authority. Membership is, of course, always a free choice. Anyone may retire at any time from such membership.[2]

2 I am aware that the kinds of responses and responsibilities I am describing above refer predominantly to churches in the Protestant sector of the church. Roman Catholic and Orthodox churches may not see things in quite the

As teachers, my wife and I have relocated often, necessitating frequent changes of church. We have lived with our family in several small, rural communities, as well as in large cities in different states. As a couple, we have lived overseas for extended periods.

We always chose a local church on the basis of its faithfulness to biblical witness, and whether it could provide suitable ministries for our whole family, including three children. We took our responsibility to bring our children up in the church very seriously. We did not concern ourselves especially with a particular denomination.

Consequently, we have been active members of a range of churches in a variety of settings, both rural and urban: Assembly of God, independent charismatic, Presbyterian, Baptist, Uniting and Anglican. We have been associated with a number of interdenominational ministries such as Scripture Union, Gideons International, RZIM, and various Christian School associations.

One of the most poignant moments I can recall, was when an 83-year-old retired missionary led the Communion service in an independent charismatic church we were attending. He had spent around 30 years in China and another 30 years in Japan, serving with an Australian denominational mission.

During all that time, he had not once presided over a Communion service in his home country, Australia. As a missionary in China and Japan, his denomination expected him to lead his converts in foreign countries in Communion, and he had done so thousands of times over his 60+ years of mission service. Because he was not ordained, however, church rules had not permitted him to do so in his denominational church within Australia.

This gracious and godly old man had tears in his eyes as he

same way. But that in itself reinforces the point that I am making.

told us of his sense of liberation that at last, in this independent church, he could lead Australian worshippers in this service of celebration of the Lord's Supper.

Vocation

In 2007, I spent some time at OCCA The Oxford Centre for Christian Apologetics in Oxford, partly to probe the minds of scholars there and at Wycliff Hall about the notion of vocation. From many authors I read then, I quote just three.

> Calling is the truth that God calls us to himself so decisively that everything we are, everything we do, and everything we have is invested with a special devotion and dynamism lived out as a response to his summons and service.[3]

When I first read this, it resonated deeply with both my spirit and my experience. Guinness argued that God's calling is not necessarily to a role, and certainly not only to roles of 'full-time Christian ministry', whatever that might mean. God's calling is to abundant life with Christ for all kinds of purposes and in all stages of life.

Life lived in service ministry to God will be a life called by God. Whatever a person does in that service ministry – whether paid or unpaid work; as a volunteer, an employed person, or under compulsion while serving a prison sentence – may be as important to God as the work of an apostle.[4]

The second reference is from C. S. Lewis, perhaps the most powerful Christian apologist of the 20th century, who eschewed any denominational emphasis or ordained role.

---

[3] Guinness, *The Call: Finding and Fulfilling the Central Purpose of Your Life*, p. 4.

[4] There is a long record of significant thinkers in the church over the millennia who have supported and promulgated the view that all work is of equivalent value, whether secular or sacred. Guinness gives a useful summary of some of these in: ibid., pp. 31–5.

He demonstrated powerfully the capacity of a professional or academic expert to aptly apply 'mere Christianity' to everyday, lay concerns.

> We can make people (often) attend to the Christian point of view for half an hour or so; but the moment they have ... laid down our article, they are plunged back into a world where the opposite position is taken for granted ... What we want is not more little books about Christianity, but more little books by Christians on other subjects – with their Christianity latent.[5]

Lewis was encouraging young people to stay in their professions, doing good work *for the sake of that work*, doing it well and becoming the best experts they could be. How wonderful, he continued, if every time you wanted to read a work on science or history or some other academic field, the best author available turned out to be a Christian! But their Christianity, he said, should be 'latent, not explicit'. And the work would have to be absolutely honest.

We hear a lot in churches about vocation or calling. Young people agonise about what it might be that God is calling them to do.[6] When careers advisers talk to people about employment options, they call this advice 'vocational guidance'. In an odd quirk of modern language shift (at least in Australia, this is the case), we now apply the description 'vocational training' to educational preparation for work in the manual trades only.

The final reference is from William Tyndale, translator of the New Testament into English early in the sixteenth century, who wrote: 'There is no work better than another to please

---

5 C. S. Lewis, *God in the Dock* (Grand Rapids, MI: William B. Eerdmans, 1970), p. 93.

6 In thinking through these issues, I always advise young people to read the best book I know on this topic: Garry Friesen, *Decision Making and the Will of God: A Biblical Alternative to the Traditional View* (Multnomah Publishers: Portland, OR, 1981).

God; to pour water, to wash dishes, to be a souter [cobbler], or an apostle, all is one; to wash dishes and to preach is all one, as touching the deed, to please God.'[7]

God appears to call people equally to what we sometimes call 'secular' work, as he does to what we call 'ministry' work. In fact, those two distinctions are utterly unknown in scripture. The first 'calling' of a person in the Bible to do God's work had nothing to do with traditional ministry work. God called a man named Bezalel to construct the tabernacle in the desert, and another man Oholiab, to make all the soft furnishings for the tabernacle.

Speaking about Bezalel, Moses said that God 'has filled him with divine Spirit, with skill, intelligence, and knowledge in every kind of craft' (Ex 35:31). Speaking about both of them, Moses added that God 'has inspired him to teach, both him and Oholiab' (Ex 35:34).

Being 'called' and *filled with the spirit of God* to work on building a tabernacle and to teach others is thus a job description 'first used, neither of a priest nor a prophet, but of an artisan, a 'blue-collar' worker. Perhaps this will give us a hint of how much God values the work of our hands.'[8] This is a foundational Old Testament teaching that the contemporary church seems to have overlooked.

Many people in 'secular' jobs describe their desire to serve God through their daily work, which they regard as a vocation.[9] The personal testimonies of the participants in my research in Chapter Two demonstrated that clearly. They all understood that they were living out in their own working lives the person

---

7 Costa, *God at Work*, pp. 24–5.

8 Richard J. Foster, *Streams of Living Water* (Bath, UK: Eagle Publishing, 1999), p. 207.

9 'We have a sense of calling, a God-given ability to do a job linked with a God-given enjoyment in doing it.' Ibid., p. 224.

of Jesus Christ who lives in them, and in whom they trust.

It is as we work as Christ in the world that we may most closely reflect the incarnated Son, who saw no inconsistency in divinity becoming human, being formed in the womb, making his life among men, women and children, working with his hands, becoming as one of us. In Jesus, the supernatural became ordinary, was transformed into a being neither solely divine nor solely human, was life-giving, creative and yet grounded.

Several of the participants in my study reported that their daily work was 'life-giving' for them. Far from being toilsome or laborious, even when their work was hard and tiring, even stressful, it gave them life. No doubt, part of that life was because they were aware that they were carrying out their service to God through that work, as his images. Perhaps part also came just because they enjoyed doing what they were made for. Preece describes this as 'mutual divine and human pleasure in work'.[10]

Living out your passion seems to be precisely what Frederic Buechner had in mind when he wrote that: 'The place God calls you to, is where your deep gladness and the world's deep hunger meet.'[11] Brueggemann, writing about the call of the prophet, Jeremiah, suggested that a call does not necessarily come as a 'datable experience'.[12] It often is more of a sense of living out one's life in a deep consistency with the purposes of God. Such a call, said Brueggemann, 'has a theonomous cast', rather than an autonomous origin. It is 'not an event, but an ongoing dynamic of a growing and powerful claim'.

---

10 Preece, *The Viability of the Vocation Tradition*, p. 7.

11 Frederick Buechner, *Wishful Thinking: A Theological ABC* (New York: Harper & Row, 1973), p. 95.

12 This, and the immediate subsequent quotations are from: Walter Brueggemann, *Hopeful Imagination: Prophetic Voices in Exile* (Philadelphia, PA: Fortress Press, 1986), p. 18.

The call-to-work and live before the face of God[13] (*coram Deo*) was reinvigorated in the Reformation through Luther's concept of *Beruf*, as he perceived the Christian vocation to both faith and work, in contrast to the common human *Stand* or station in life.[14] He perceived that whether we work at this job or that is immaterial. Luther taught that 'every job, not just that of the priest or monk, is a calling, something committed to us by God, a charge laid upon us by God.'[15]

In the contemporary era, we expect careers to change constantly. Young people are constantly reminded that many of the jobs they will do in their lives have not yet been invented. Regardless of changing social conditions, however, God's primary call to humanity to work remains unchanged. The church must be careful lest it allows its language of vocation to be stuck in an age that is past. While the truth of vocation may not change, the language and concepts used to describe it must.

For the Hebrew, working for God meant working for humankind, and the reverse applied also. This is the fundamental story of Esther – doing God's work by working within and for the human world as though God did not exist.

The book of Esther is remarkable, of course, as the only book in the Bible that never mentions God – not even once. God is apparently 'absent' from the world of Esther and Mordechai, and has left human beings in charge. Of course, God is never truly absent from anywhere – in this sense the story is an extended parable.

Esther, the book, plays this concept out 'as though God were

---

13 James K. A. Smith, "Naturalizing "Shalom": Confessions of a Kuyperian Secularist," *Cardus* (June 28, 2013), https://www.cardus.ca/comment/article/3993/naturalizing-shalom-confessions-of-a-kuyperian-secularist/.

14 Gustaf Wingren, *Luther on Vocation*, trans. Carl C. Rasmussen (Eugene, OR: Wipf & Stock, 2004), p. 2.

15 Hart, "The Teaching of Luther and Calvin About Ordinary Work: 1. Martin Luther (1483–1546)," p. 44.

absent'. It is the book that most clearly describes how human beings are to live out their task of work as images of God, in place of God, to achieve justice and to create shalom.[16] Like Frodo, in *The Lord of the Rings*, we need to hear the message: 'All we have to decide is what to do with the time that is given us.'[17]

Remembering that we have been given a vice-regal task in our calling to live as images of God, working in the world *in imago Dei*, we may read the best-known verse in Esther with a personal interest: *What if you have been given your royal responsibility, your Letters Patent, for just exactly this time in history in which you have been born?* (Esth 4:14, my paraphrase).

We are to use the gifts and skills God has given us, working within whatever world system we are placed, to bring about God's justice and shalom. Scripture sets forth what is true, good and beautiful in human society – but it is left to human beings to work and contend for these outcomes. 'Man may still see God's justice and peace brought into being in the world, but it will not be handed to him; he will have to build it.'[18]

Sacred–secular distinctions

It is probably fair to state that there is a long tradition in Christian circles that having a vocation or a calling is mainly relevant to that which is often called 'full-time Christian ministry'.[19] This

16 See, for an extended discussion of this concept: Graham Leo, "Reading the Book of Esther: A Theology of Work for the 21st Century in the West," *Zadok* Summer, no. 133 (2016).

17 J. R. R. Tolkien, *The Lord of the Rings* (London: HarperCollins, 2002), p. 50.

18 Yoram Hazony, *God and Politics in Esther* (New York: Cambridge University Press, 2016), pp. 170–1.

19 This view is reflected in the Thirty-Nine Articles of the Church of England: 'It is not lawful for any man to take upon him the office of public preaching, or ministering the Sacraments in the Congregation, before he be lawfully called, and sent to execute the same.' M. D. Fraser and I. J. Gordon, "Organic Matter

view may be breaking down in our more democratic age, however. Barna's research in 2018 addressed this issue:

> Barna asked whether it was better for a Christian to become a pastor or a missionary, or to represent his faith well at work. In general, Christians are more likely to say that neither one is superior to the other (64%). After all, almost two-thirds of employed Christians (64%) agree on some level that it's clear to them how their own work serves God or a higher purpose.[20]

Frederick Buechner's statement that 'The place God calls you to, is where your deep gladness and the world's deep hunger meet,'[21] could be the starting point for a notion of vocation or call that becomes central to how Christians think about 'full-time Christian ministry'. That ministry will take most outside of church boundaries, into the worlds of commerce, industry, politics and civics.

The view taken throughout this book is that all work that does not conflict with God's character (that is, human stewardship consistent with the word-and-will of God) is of no less value than that which is commonly known as full-time Christian ministry, precisely because it is the 'administration' of viceroys. The old chestnut of 'full-time Christian service', usually used to subtly denigrate 'secular' (i.e. less spiritual) work, is a foreign concept in the Hebrew scriptures.[22]

Of course, this does not negate the value of a vocation serving God in the church. It would be taking this notion too far to assume that one could not be called to service as a pastor or priest just as much as another is called to service as a doctor

---

Intake, Diet Digestibility and Feeding Behaviour of Goats, Red Deer, and South American Camelids Feeding on Three Contrasting Scottish Vegetation Communities.," *Journal of Applied Ecology* 34 (1997). Article 23.

20 "Christians at Work: Examining the Intersection of Calling and Career."

21 Buechner, *Wishful Thinking: A Theological ABC*, p. 95.

22 Hazony, *God and Politics in Esther*, pp. 149–50.

or a carpenter. Let me hasten to clarify that this book, and this chapter, is not seeking to deny ordination.

Just as doctors and carpenters have to be licensed by an appropriate body, so should pastors and priests. Let's not allow language terms to get in the way. Plumbers are licensed; teachers are registered; accountants are certified; priests are ordained. The point I am making over and over here, is that the notion of vocation should not be limited to the church; that full-time Christian service is not limited to service in the church.

Stevens[23] and Hardy[24] have both written extensively on this topic, building a careful body of argument to propose the sacredness of all work done to the glory of God. Grasping this perspective would free us from the 'spiritual schizophrenia that splits the world too neatly into categories of sacred and profane: ... Eucharist is a holy supper. The dinner ...on the kitchen table isn't. A group of nuns is holy. The office project team isn't.'[25]

The medieval classic describing how the monk, Brother Lawrence, viewed all of his daily, menial tasks through a vocational lens is certainly indicative of how this view predates modernist thought, even if it were not a common response.[26]

Some people will object to all of this, saying that they just 'know' that God called them to this or that particular work, either 'ministry' or 'secular'. The general line of argument we

---

23 R. Paul Stevens, *The Abolition of the Laity: Vocation, Work, and Ministry in Biblical Perspective* (Carlisle, UK: Paternoster, 1999).

24 Lee Hardy, *The Fabric of This World: Inquiries into Calling, Career Choice, and the Design of Human Work* (Grand Rapids, MI: William. B. Eerdmans, 1990).

25 Alice Camille, "Hope for Monday Mornings " *U.S. Catholic* 80, no. 2 (Feb.1, 2015): p. 46.

26 *The Practice of the Presence of God*, trans. E. M. Blaiklock (London: Hodder and Stoughton, 1981).

have been following does not rule out the possibility that some work may come about as a result of what has been called 'divine discontent',[27] even if others may simply make a choice to work at what they simply enjoy most and are best at.

We do not live in a closed universe, away from God's influence on us. God may sometimes be somehow involved in *inspiring*, even if not *ordaining* the work we do, but the line of distinction between ordinary work and that which is inspired may remain unclear, at least in this life. The difference may be more in the spiritual perceptiveness of the person doing the work than the work itself.

Messenger[28] pointed out that not more than about a hundred people were called by God in the Bible to a particular job, and these were usually to very notable positions or at significant points in history, e.g. Noah, Paul, Samuel, Bezalel. In scripture, God appears to call people equally to what we sometimes call 'secular' work, as he does to what we call 'ministry' work.

It is worth quoting at length two voices, who both spoke strongly to this question, each demanding that all attempts to declare some work as sacred, and some as secular, be set aside for ever:

The unbiblical use of the terms 'ministry' and 'laity' is the most extensive and oppressive form of exclusive language

---

27 'The phrase comes from a vocations handbook and is used when God is stirring someone up, making them a bit uncomfortable to teach them something, interrupting their everyday life with a new direction or way of thinking.' Canon Dr Graham Dodds, "Finding Rest," (Sermon preached at Wells Cathedral, Evensong 12 October, 2014). Canon Dodds kindly sent me a copy of his sermon after the service, following our conversation on the thoughts he had inspired in me during the service.

28 Will Messenger, "Gifts That Differ; Callings That Unite. An Interview with Will Messenger," *Christian History Institute*, no. 110 (2014). He noted that 'everyone is called to belong to Christ and to participate in his creative and redemptive work' but that it is 'rare for God to call someone directly and unmistakably to particular work'.

in the church. When we use gender-exclusive language, we exclude about 50% of all Christians. But when we use the minister/layperson distinction, we exclude 90–95% of all Christians. (Howard Snyder.)[29]

Christian people, and particularly perhaps the Christian clergy, must get it firmly into their heads that when a man or woman is called to a particular job of secular work, that is as true a vocation as though he or she were called to specifically religious work. (Dorothy Sayers.)[30]

If church leaders understood and accepted these principles, they could not fail to give their lay members 'the perspective that their job really matters to their faith'.[31]

It is perhaps not an unreasonable conclusion that one of the main reasons for the frequent failure to do so is that there is an implicit understanding that the main life of the church happens on Sunday as the weekly church service is under way. Most clergy would probably disavow this notion in theory, but common practice seems to reflect it.

The truth is that *the church dispersed* into the workplaces of the city and nation is just as much the church at work and worship as is *the church gathered* on Sunday.

---

29 Howard Snyder, *Global Good News* (Nashville, TN: Abingdon Press, 2001), p. 230. Cited in Russell, "The Secret of Marketplace Leadership Success: Constructing a Comprehensive Framework for the Effective Integration of Leadership, Faith, and Work," p. 90.

30 Sayers, *Letters to a Diminished Church*, p. 138.

31 Russell, "The Secret of Marketplace Leadership Success: Constructing a Comprehensive Framework for the Effective Integration of Leadership, Faith, and Work," p. 74. (This was a research-based conclusion, not merely an assertion.)

CHAPTER SIX

How Can My Work Become Worship?

A theology of work to take into your workplace or lifeplace

It is important to stress that when we talk about work, we are not only talking about paid work. Work, as we now understand it in its biblical context and purpose, includes volunteer work. It includes the work of carers in the home, the learning and studying undertaken by little children as well as by university students, and the ordinary daily activities of housework, gardening and managing our family, social and economic lives.

A definition of work

All of these kinds of human activity are reflected in *my definition of work*, which we will examine further in the course of this chapter:

> *Work is any means by which we navigate or sustain our way in the world, as creatures reflecting God's vocational instruction-blessing to be rulers, obediently exercising God's authority in the universe on God's behalf.*

The definition uses the word *vocational* (Latin, *vocare*: to call) because this reflects the original call-to-work of creatures made *in imago Dei* in the creation narratives. It acknowledges the choices that we make towards God, in a world and society recalcitrant to the word-and-will of God. It affirms all activity that sustains, nurtures and creatively develops the world, society and the individual. We will also address (below) that 'work' that expends energy in life-destructive activity done *against* the word-and-will of God.

The *instruction-blessing* of ruling, of taking charge, of administering, so important in my definition, is drawn from Genesis 1:28: *God blessed them, and God said to them, "Be **fruitful** and multiply, and fill the earth and **subdue** it; **and have dominion [rule]** over the fish of the sea and over the birds of the air, and over every living thing that moves upon the earth."*

The three verbs highlighted in bold type need to be carefully noted. They will appear again and again in this chapter.

It will be helpful to read this definition of work in the light of the following summary of our learning thus far.

1. Work is essential to the very nature and purpose of humankind.[1]

2. Work is given to humankind as a royal task. This is the universal human vocation (i.e. calling). Humans are to act *in imago Dei*, acting as God's viceroys – ruling, stewarding and managing the earth, as God would.

3. The advent of the incarnate Son, Jesus Christ, does not remove or supplant our role as workers stewarding the earth in God's image. On the contrary, it empowers it; it redefines it for the kingdom age. Jesus role-modelled for us the task of ruling, of being in the true image of God.

   Our mode for ruling, following the advent of Jesus, is drawn from his model of the Obedient human, the suffering, self-sacrificing *servant of God*, the *ebed Yahweh*. The work of those who lived *before* the advent of Jesus was essentially obedience to God by humans seeking to honour and obey the Sovereign Lord. Our work *after* Christ continues that former role, but adds obedient service to, and modelling of life upon, the

---

1 'Work is regarded as an essential part of man's state not only in the Creation narrative, but in the whole of the Old Testament. A life without work would not be a complete life; it would be an existence quite unworthy of man.' Claus Westermann, *Creation*, trans. John J. Scullion (London: SPCK, 1974), p. 81.

Son who worked both with tools and words, and also performed his ultimate work on the cross.

Further, our work is done in service to a King, not quite so much *in absentia* as for our Old Testament brothers and sisters. Although Jesus has 'gone away', he has promised to be with us, 'always', through the indwelling presence of the Holy Spirit.

Still further, we who live after Christ's first advent, now look forward in confident hope (based on Rev 22:3–5), to a new mode or role of ruling that will be given to redeemed humankind as part of the new heavens and new earth. At that time, however, the King will not be *in absentia*, but rather very present. Our rule will then be in *partnership*, not as *viceroys*. It is this to which all our work now looks forward.

4. Human beings have the free choice to respond in obedience to, or to reject the word-and-will of God. Our capacity to do so fully, however, is always threatened by the power of the world system, our personal circumstances, our egos and our spiritual inclinations.[2] All of these make us inherently likely to disobey.

5. Work always entails activity in one or more of the three areas of (a) *fruitfulness*, i.e. creating or affirming life; (b) *subduing*, i.e. controlling or managing, converting to noble human purposes, removing resistance; or (c) *ruling*, i.e. exercising rightful control as viceroys, ruling for the King *in absentia*.

   Thus no work that is obedient to the word-and-will of God is of more or less value than any other, or more or less 'spiritual' than any other. The work of cleaners,

---

2 Westermann probes this dilemma in ibid., pp. 91–2.

teachers, ministers and accountants is of equal value –
and all paid work is of equal value to unpaid work.

6. Work itself does *not* need to be redeemed because it
is, from its original sacred beginning, human activity,
blessed and ordained by God. It is *not* cursed, any more
than eating, trading or any other human activity that
might be done for good or ill.

This is not to say that everything in our garden is rosy.
We freely acknowledge that the physical structures of
the world and all creatures in creation are groaning and
waiting for the good work of restoration/renewal that
will come in God's good time (Rom 8:19–22).

This renewal has already been modelled in deed and
word, by the only truly obedient man, '… the chosen
one, who according to Isaiah 53 brings the salvation of
God to the wicked, is designated as worker, 'servant of
God', *ebed Yahweh*'.[3]

7. The vocation (calling) of all human beings as we work
within the world system, corrupted though it is by
selfishness and abuse of power, is to bring the products
of our minds and hands to God, both as first-fruits and
as worship.[4]

We stand as rulers and priests between God and the
entire creation, in reflection of the One who mediated
between us and God, 'bringing God's wise and
generous order to the world and giving articulate voice
to creation's glad and grateful praise to its maker'.[5]

3 Moltmann, *On Human Dignity: Political Theology and Ethics*, p. 42.
4 ' "Good work to do" is but another name for worship.' Stanley Hauerwas,
Matthew, ed. R. R. Reno, Brazos Theological Commentary on the Bible
(Grand Rapids, MI: Brazos Press, 2006), p.141.
5 N. T. Wright, *Virtue Reborn* (London: SPCK, 2010), p. 70–1.

Witnessing at work

I mentioned very briefly in the introduction that I have noticed a tendency for churches and some writers/speakers to encourage Christians to 'take their faith into the workplace' by witnessing for Christ to their colleagues. This practice is sometimes promoted as a way of 'being a Christian at work'.

I am not going to argue against that practice, as long as it is not done by stealing company time (both the witnesser's *and* the 'victim's' paid time); *and* as long as it does not constitute religious harassment. This latter can be an especial risk if the Christian doing the witnessing is in a superior position of rank or power to the other party. Because there are so many risks of misinterpretation, however, I must confess to a certain sense of discomfort about recommending this as a good practice, unless a person is actually asked about their faith.

But even if such witnessing were well done, it would have almost nothing to do with bringing our Christian faith properly into the workplace. A far better Christian witness comes from our consistent character in the workplace.

Read the comments of the people in my research, in Chapter Two. Over and over they speak about doing their jobs really well, because that is what counts. They are concerned for leaving a legacy, for having a sound reputation, for simply doing the tasks in their Position Description well. One was deeply concerned that he leave a legacy in the Public Health system – hardly something that anyone will ever be able to track in such a vast complex as State Public Health. Yet he was confident that this was a good work (or a good worship) to do for God.

Bringing faith into work, worshipping while working, has very little to do with trying to persuade colleagues or clients to become Christians. It has a great deal to do with living and working as though one is Christ, 'making good tables'.

Work done in obedience

The royal command of God to work is not limited to Christians. God has always used pagan nations, foreign leaders and ordinary people outside of the nation of Israel (in the Old Testament) or the community of Christian faith (in the New Testament) to achieve his purposes. Thus, as Volf and others agree, the work of those who do not choose to serve God is still capable of being appropriated by him to achieve his ends, if that work is consistent with the tasks of an *imago Dei,* an image of God, doing God's work for him.[6]

Genuine work is obedient response to the primary command of God, in Genesis 1:28, repeated in the Fourth Commandment[7] after the people of God were delivered from Egypt, and re-stated by Jesus.[8] This genuine work may be done by Christians *and* by non-believers, as each works honourably in accordance with God's created purpose. The work of replenishing, subduing and taking dominion will always be in keeping with Christ's salvific mission for the world – including the earth itself.

This sense of obedience to a divine call in ordinary, day-to-day matters was precisely expressed by Bonhoeffer, writing from prison to his fiancée: 'Our marriage shall be a *yes* to God's earth; it shall strengthen our courage to act and accomplish something on the earth.'[9] This unity of divine and human

---

6 Volf, pp. 118ff.

7 Ex 20:8–11. Abraham Joshua Heschel noted, 'Just as we are commanded to keep Sabbath, we are commanded to labour. The duty to work for six days is just as much a part of God's covenant with man as to abstain from work on the seventh day.' Abraham Joshua Heschel, *The Sabbath* (New York: Noonday Press, 1979), p. 28.

8 Jn 4:35; Mt 28:18–20.

9 Geffrey B. Kelly and F. Burton Nelson, eds., *A Testament to Freedom: The Essential Writings of Dietrich Bonhoeffer* (San Francisco: Harper, 1990), p. 512.

purposes resolves the dilemma of vocation as a mystery that is neither secular nor spiritual, and yet both, as discussed above.

It was also beautifully encompassed in the diary of Dag Hammarskjöld, the Secretary-General of the United Nations, whose life was tragically cut short in an air disaster:

> I don't know Who – or what – put the question. I don't know when it was put. I don't even remember answering. But at some moment I did answer *Yes* to Someone – or Something – and from that hour I was certain that existence is meaningful and that, therefore, my life, in self-surrender, had a goal.[10]

Ultimately, all good work is sustained by Jesus Christ as Lord of the harvest. Work that does not honour him is of evil origin. Like wheat and tares, 'the Creator's work and humanity's disobedience'[11] continue to exist in tension in the present.

Work that serves God draws upon the Creator's provisioning, energising power, regardless of who performs it. God's sustaining and transformative power is at work at all times, in the cycle of the seasons, the germination of seeds, the control of history, the achievement of God's own *telos* known only to the Trinity in its fullness.

This principle for the understanding of how our daily work serves his purposes is poetically summarised in Psalm 127:1–2.

> *Unless the* LORD *builds the house,*
> *those who build it labour in vain.*
> *Unless the* LORD *guards the city,*
> *the guard keeps watch in vain.*
> *It is vain that you rise up early,*
> *and go late to rest,*

---

10 Dag Hammarskjold, *Markings*, trans. Leif Sjoberg and W. H. Auden (New York: Alfred A. Knopf, 1969), p. 205. (Hammarskjold was a highly respected Secretary-General of the United Nations, and was also a Christian.)
11 Larive, *After Sunday: A Theology of Work*, p. 11.

> *eating the bread of anxious toil;*
> *for he gives sleep to his beloved.*

This is why all work is *vocational* – God's calling is confirmed in his answering-by-provision. If the work is anti-God, then he does not sustain it – the work is 'in vain'.[12]

We may be a multinational CEO, a brain surgeon, a hairdresser or a tyre-repairer. We may be paid for our work, or we may be a volunteer. Our work may be caring for an invalid relative. Or our work may be just living day-to-day in our own house as an aged or disabled person, making our meals, cleaning the floors and toilets and making the most we can of our life.

What matters is whether we do it to the best of our capacity. It matters that we do it with the express intention of ruling, organising, taking management of our environment as the one to whom God has given this little bit of the universe to look after. It even matters if you have no such noble intention, but nevertheless do good work that reflects what human beings were created to do. Millions of generally good people who are not Christians do this every day.

This principle also helps us with the vexed question of how we are to deal with dull or boring jobs. It cannot fairly be denied that some people, often through no fault of their own, through their socio-economic background, are forced to work in roles that are not particularly exciting.

It would be unfair and absurdly 'super-spiritual', to suggest that these folk should just make the best of it, praising the Lord while they work. While there may be some value in that advice, there must be more that one can do to help those in such situations. I think there is. (Of course, seeking to change

---

12 The Hebrew for 'in vain' here is *shua*; the same root as in the name *Yeshua (Jesus: God saves)*. *Shua* is essentially a cry for help, a plea for salvation.

one's job is an option that may be open to us.)

We must simply come back to first principles. We are human creatures, called to do vice-regal tasks in the name of the Most High God. Service to him requires that we simply do our work with the attitude that we are doing something very important for God's kingdom. If this work were not done, what would happen? Presumably some essential human need would not be met.

Once we recognise that we are meeting a need by our work, even if we don't enjoy it, we can do it as though we were doing it to God. But a special note to employers here! It is incumbent on employers and managers to give regard and commendation to all workers at all levels of an organisation.

I read the following delightful anecdote in a journal once. The writer was being toured around a secondary college. He had noticed that the college had a large number of plaques and memorials dedicated to people who had worked there:

> 'You should see the James Matthews memorial plaque,' suggested Mr William Braithwaite, a tutor. I did. The first lines read, 'Reliable, conscientious and professional in performance of his duties, immensely strong and spiritual in character, with genuine and loving concern for his fellow man and the College.' I asked about Matthews. 'He worked as a janitor in the college for thirty years,' Mr Braithwaite replied. 'He was very proud of his work, knew who he was, and what he wanted from life.' What kind of college celebrates the life of a janitor?[13]

The janitor may not have needed affirmation from his employer to know that his work mattered. But his employer needed to affirm his employee's work because that was what mattered *in the manager's work.*

---

13 Miguel Monjardino, "A Liberal Education," *City Journal* Autumn (2013).

Summary of my theology of work

Work is any means by which we navigate or sustain our way in the world, as creatures reflecting God's vocational instruction-blessing to be rulers, obediently exercising God's authority in the universe on God's behalf.

This definition reflects the original call-to-work of creatures made *in imago Dei* in the creation narratives. It acknowledges the choices that we make towards or away from God, in a world and society recalcitrant to the word-and-will of God.

On the other hand, this definition affirms all activity that sustains, nurtures and creatively develops the world, society and the individual. It includes *your* work – whatever that work is – as long as it is being fruitful, subduing or ruling, as God would do if he were here in *your* place!

Now that the kingdom of God has been inaugurated, though not yet consummated, in the advent of the Lord Jesus Christ, we work with even greater clarity of purpose, and with greater sense of the self-sacrifice that is required of us. Our 'desire is towards him'.

Work is human homework set by God, first at creation, redefined by Jesus, and empowered by the Holy Spirit. Human work in its truest form serves God in true humility, and is enabled, blessed and inspired by God; it is neither self-need–serving, nor world system–serving.

Descriptions of work that focus on work-as-burdensome-toil due to God's alleged curse fail to glimpse the delight and glory of the vocation given to humankind. More importantly, they fail to acknowledge the high calling of humankind to serve as a viceroy to the Most High God.

True happiness does not reside in leisure from work, but in the confident performance of our work as humans made a little lower than heavenly beings, but crowned with glory and honour, given vice-regal dominion over the works of God's hand (Ps 8:4–8).

Our best work will often be indistinguishable from play, because we enjoy what we do, being free to cooperate with God in the work that we do and to use our gifts to the best advantage. Even children may work, within this definition, as they order their world in play and learning, as they live and act in obedience, first to their parents in the sovereign order of creation, and then to God.

All of us, whatever our vocation, whether we work as lawyers or ministers, as business owners or employees, as labourers or volunteers, may enjoy the simple pleasure of serving the God who called us to be workers, in his own image.

Our work *is* our worship.

Our obedience is our response to his gift of life.

Our joyful building of the future kingdom through our daily work is our worshipful response to the sacrifice of the True Servant-Worker of God, the *ebed Yahweh*, the Son of God, the Lord Jesus Christ.

CHAPTER SEVEN
Bringing Work to Church

**Suggestions for the local church to engage with
the work lives of their congregation members**

I've attended church all my life. Apart from when prevented
by illness or some other serious impediment, I suppose I
have missed very few Sunday mornings at my local church.
My reasons for attending have been mixed: my duty to God,
my desire to worship, my training of my children, but also
partly a sense of responsibility to the wider community (Paul
called this the 'body') of the church. All of these, I think, are
consistent with scripture.

In regard to the first two reasons, nothing whatever can
be demanded by me or expected by me. The attention is all
directed one way – from me to God. Any return to me is sheer
grace, not merit. The third reason relates to my duty as a parent
before God. But the fourth? If each Christian has an obligation
to the body, does not the body also have an obligation to the
individual member? I take it for granted that God has no
obligations to any of us!

Is it reasonable that the community, the *ekklesia*, the body
of believers who meet at a particular rural, suburban or city
address, should encourage the members to bring something of
their own selves into their meeting together? Paul encourages
us not to give up meeting together. He writes about the
fellowship, the *koinonia* of meeting. All of this implies some
sense of knowing each other beyond the 'Say hello to someone
as you sit down,' which is the very 'low church' equivalent of

saying, 'The peace of the Lord be with you.'

I suggested in the very first chapter that our working lives form a core element of who we are. If, theologically, as we now understand having read this far, our work is our central calling as human beings, how should our coming together as community acknowledge our work lives?

This question will form the core of this final chapter.

The disturbing demographics of church attendance

Church attendance by both men and women across the West is in decline. For reasons of space, I present only brief snippets of Australian data, but the Australian picture has similarities with trends in the UK, the USA and across Europe. There is clear evidence of declining attendance in Australian churches of all kinds, with fewer than 20% of the population attending at least once a month.[1]

Very few Australian studies have examined the church–work connection. We do know that for occasional or non-attenders at church, by far the most common reason for not attending is that 'it is irrelevant to my life.'[2]

Further, we know that about 23% of regular church attenders have university degrees (compared with 13% of all Australians over 15 years).[3] Thus, almost twice as many church attenders

---

[1] NCLS research http://www.ncls.org.au/default.aspx?sitemapid=23.

[2] 47% give this reason, against the next most common reasons: 'Don't accept how it's taught' (26%) and 'Outdated style' (24%). The McCrindle Blog, "Church Attendance in Australia (Infographic) 2013," McCrindle, http://www.mccrindle.com.au/the-mccrindle-blog/church_attendance_in_australia_infographic.

[3] I have not addressed this high proportion of church attenders with a tertiary education in this discussion. However, it is reasonable to assume that almost one quarter of church attenders are used to thinking at a fairly high order, and in abstract terms. How might knowledge of this fact affect how church leaders structure services?

hold tertiary qualifications than in the general population.

A brief review of National Church Life Survey statistics reveals that our churches contain fewer men than women; that there is a skewing towards an older (and probably retired or semiretired) population in churches; that church attenders are generally better educated and thus possibly more likely to be analytical and thoughtful than the general population.

It is worth asking whether, or how often, at Parish Council meetings, Elders meetings, or similar gatherings, there is pause to consider the known demographics and characteristics of the congregations and local communities. Would some things be done differently if they did know more about their congregations' level of education, socio-economic status, job circumstances, and so on?

What could churches do differently?

The following suggestions are drawn predominantly from the comments of the research participants whom I interviewed, only occasionally enhanced with my own additions. In fact, well over 90% of the actual words and ideas come directly from my research participants.

The list is subdivided into headings for practicality. It is intended to be useful to a wide range of people who may be involved in planning Christian church services of various kinds.

Two disclaimers or caveats are in order:

First, nothing in this list should detract from a church's full focus on God, and worship of Jesus Christ, in gathered settings. These suggestions are not a call to human-centred celebration of life, or humanistic dilution of orthodox Christian worship. Any such temptation should be carefully avoided. They are, rather, a call to centre our worship on God by bringing our lives and our physical beings into his presence (Rom 12:1) and acknowledging the evidence of God's presence in daily work.

Second, these are *suggestions,* not a list of demands. This is not an attempt to usurp the rightful authority of church leaders or denominational traditions regarding the structure and content of corporate worship. I hope the language in which they are couched will make this quite clear.

All of these suggestions are made with the hope that thoughtful church leaders will prayerfully reflect on them, engage with others in discussion, and perhaps make considered changes within the gathered practices of the church.

Ultimately, those who attend church will form their own judgements and, as the media like to say, vote with their feet. My hope is that if some churches take up some of these suggestions, they will find that their churches not only grow numerically, but also spiritually.

What churches could teach

1. Church ministers and leaders could ensure that they have a clear theology about the nature of work and its place in human purpose. The seven summary points I made about work at the beginning of Chapter Six would be a good place to start.

2. Churches could regularly and frequently teach congregations about the nature of work and its place in human purpose. The research that I conducted demonstrated a low level of such understanding among most congregation members who had been attending church for a long period of time and who were generally well educated. It is likely that this would be replicated if conducted across a wider sample.

3. Work should be carefully defined so as to consciously

and clearly include all kinds of volunteer and unpaid work, including day-to-day domestic and carer types of work, which will probably be very common in most congregations.

4. Churches could teach that day-to-day work is not primarily for the purpose of evangelism; it is to do the best possible job in the work tasks required of us, which is, in itself, a gospel witness.[4] People need to be taught to enjoy and see value in work that appears to be uninspiring. Nor should teaching on work be reduced to encouraging desirable behaviours, such as integrity and kindness.

5. Churches could teach young people how to properly value their natural gifts, taking full advantage of educational opportunities to develop those gifts to the maximum. Too many young people who have talent for science, business, or media are drawn away from their area of gifting to perform 'full-time Christian service' as interns, or to take up short-term roles in 'Christian mission'. These may result in permanent loss of earlier career goals.

The church ought to be a major producer of business leaders, politicians, highly qualified scientists and technicians. (The church was, after all, the birthplace of modern science.[5] Too many young people in church are discouraged from science by fears that it might somehow conflict with their understanding of the Bible.[6])

---

[4] This is a logical corollary of 1 Pet 3:15.

[5] This point is argued at length in: Peter Harrison, "Religion, the Royal Society, and the Rise of Science," *Theology and Science* 6, no. 3 (2008).

[6] Krista Bontrager, "Inspiring the Next Generation of Scientists," 12 February (2015), http://www.reasons.org/articles/Inspiring-the-Next-Generation-of-Scientists.

What church services could include

6. Churches could give opportunities for workers to tell stories about their work and their lives at work. As part of church services, people from the pews could be sharing their stories, telling their testimonies of why they do the work they do, or what has happened in the previous week.

    The focus should not be on triumphant tales of evangelism or 'little miracles that happened to me this week', but instead encourage the truthful, warts-and-all telling and hearing of ordinary, unmiraculous, faithful, sometimes difficult and dispiriting work that was done in the past week for the good of God's world. Triumphalism should be avoided – such a time of honest sharing should not be allowed to be gazumped by those who want to boast of their claimed spiritual successes, advertise their business, or pretend they have a hot-line to God, who always helps them miraculously. Nothing would close down the kinds of sharing being sought faster than these behaviours.

    Sales achieved, research completed, business managed, including failures and struggles – all these encourage others to know that they are not alone in serving God in their work lives amidst both triumphs and struggles.

    Those workers who might think their work doesn't matter much – some tradespeople, labourers, bus drivers, cleaners – could be equally encouraged to share images or stories of their work. They may need to be reminded: it is the work that is being celebrated, not its glamour or perceived 'value'; and not the opportunities taken to 'share the gospel'. Volunteers, unpaid carers and domestic workers should also be included.

Shared stories allow others to glimpse something of the presence of God *outside* the church building. They enable people to see God's kingdom coming in ways that look nothing like singing, praying or preaching. Stories told by congregation members who are doing things outside of the influence and control of the church enable people to see the presence of God in the lives of believers in dispersion.

7. Such stories can be on video – they do not need to be live presentations. For many people, a pre-recorded interview is a less traumatic way of speaking to a large audience. It is also possible in a carefully edited three minute clip to show large numbers of congregation members at work in their work environments, wearing their work clothes.

   Pre-recorded stories present a far more economical use of time within the confines of a church service. There are probably young people or part-time workers who would be happy to go out to workplaces to film such activity and edit it for Sunday viewing.

8. Ministers could map and analyse the timing, structures, and content of services to confirm how much emphasis is actually given to affirmation of attenders' work lives. Detailed analysis of service content and structure can reveal patterns and emphases that do not actually reflect the intentions held by church leaders. Retired engineers might do a particularly fine job of this.

9. Planned liturgical readings, responses and prayers that specifically honour and reflect the working lives of all members of the congregation help to affirm the placing of a high value on work.

   Liturgy is, of course, derived from two Greek words:

laos: people and *ergon*: work. The liturgical work of the people in celebrating their work completes the circle of their work-as-worship. There are online models available for adaptation.[7]

The 'farmer's prayer'[8] in Deuteronomy 26:5–10 is a magnificent model that could be adapted for all kinds of work-related celebrations, ceremonies and prayers in church services.

10. Corporate prayers could be offered in matters of direct relevance to Australian workers and workplaces in general, not just those represented in the pews: thanks could be offered for share market successes or global trade deals struck in the past week; intercessions offered for those in medical or technical research, law-making and law-enforcing; confessions articulated for white collar crime or exploitation of workers.

Finding renewed joy and satisfaction in the actual work of congregation members could be a major focus. Imagine if a newcomer came to church only to hear that the congregation were praying in earnest for the success of a local metal-fabricating factory or for all mechanics and engineering workers in that city.

All those people who said church was irrelevant to their needs, might rapidly change their tune if they were to hear such prayers. That's evangelism, without even trying!

7 See, for example: "Connecting Liturgy with Life – an Extract," The London Institute for Contemporary Christianity, http://www.licc.org.uk/resources/connecting-liturgy-with-life-an-extract/. or "Litany for the Workplace," Centre for Faith and Work, http://www.centerforfaithandwork.com/node/789?utm_source=MMM+1st+January+2015&utm_campaign=MMM+1-8-15&utm_medium=email.

8 This is the title given to this lovely prayer in: Walter Zimmerli, *Old Testament Theology in Outline* (Edinburgh: T. & T. Clark Ltd, 1978), p. 68.

11. Each church could affirm Christians in the time they commit to the daily work that they do. Members need not be pressured with guilt feelings, or made to feel greater expectations and obligations when they are already struggling to make time for family and church life. Members could be affirmed in their daily work as their worship and contribution to the kingdom of God.

12. Celebrations of work that encourage members to bring in their tools or work-products, in a contemporary re-working of ancient Harvest Festivals could be on the church's planned calendar – and not just once a year. A model of how a church might structure such a calendar is attached as an Appendix.

    If a church were to follow my suggested calendar, they would cover every possible occupation in their congregation at least once a year. They would only need to spend about ten minutes one Sunday a month in doing this. This is not a lot to ask of a church for a potentially enormous gain.

How churches might engage with the 21st century

13. Churches could take into account the changing patterns of work in our era[9]: more complicated work–life balances, less manual work but more theoretical work, longer or different work-hours and days, shift work, fly-in–fly-out work, work that operates in constant global interactivity … Each church could think about how to recognise and honour these types of work changes within their own congregation.

---

9 See Chapter One for a brief exposition of some likely changes to the structure of work in our society. Local conditions that relate to the local church would be even more relevant.

14. More and more people are engaged in lifelong education: work-related improvement and general self-education. Education is a form of work, as human beings respond obediently to the call of God to steward the world. The church could find ways to honour and value learning of all kinds and at all levels.

Imagine going to your workplace's professional development seminar, knowing that last Sunday your church prayed for all companies doing professional development this month.

How churches could foster work-based community

15. Churches could change the centre of gravity of church life away from clergy and employed staff to the people in the pews. While maintaining the focus on worship of God in gathered settings, engagement with the people's work lives can enhance that worship.

16. The church could find ways to support mentoring from within its members for the benefit of its members. Small groups based around people who work in similar areas may benefit some, especially younger workers.

Church structures and formal practices

17. Churches could consciously manage the 'ministry' language of the church. 'Ministry' need not be reserved for activity that is within the geography or under the supervisory control of the church. Churches could seek to dismantle the hierarchy of callings and vocations, both in theory and practice.

If this is too much of a challenge for the present in some churches, then at least ministers and priests within those churches strongly wedded to this hierarchy could hold the public demonstration of that hierarchy more lightly and with greater flexibility.

18. Churches could find mechanisms for organic ideas to be brought to the surface, debated and translated into initiatives easily and smoothly. The idea that the person in the pew does not have anything to offer the church in planning and visioning could be demolished.

19. The roles of elders or church councils could be rewritten to include active pastoring of members as workers rather than as Sunday attenders.

20. Senior ministers could endeavour to access the corporate wisdom available in the pews and not just engage the ministry team. Many churches hold significant wealth of higher education, corporate wisdom and experience of which churches could well take advantage.

Church leaders might be very surprised at how many of their congregation members meet for coffee after church somewhere, and shake their heads as they reflect on how much better something could have been done 'if they had only asked me for some advice; I do that for a living'.

Beyond the local church

21. Churches could access and make available to members a wide range of global Christian resources. These could be made available via church websites, apps or other means.[10]

---

[10] One useful site could be the Oikonomia Network site. This website asserts on its home page that it is dedicated to 'helping pastors equip people for whole-life discipleship, fruitful work and economic wisdom'.

22. The Global Leadership Summit sponsored by the Willow Creek Association was frequently referenced by my research participants as a valuable resource event. Such events can engage people not only within the church but also draw civic and business leaders into the church environment.

Ministerial practice

23. Ministers and clergy could ensure that they maintain their own professional development in theology, and are up to date with theological ideas that are more thoroughly researched than the material presented in many popular Christian books.

24. Ministers could ensure that there is an avenue for those who value intellectual life to find opportunities to explore complex issues from a Christian perspective.

    As more and more people in the pews hold tertiary qualifications, churches could move beyond simplistic expressions and publications, and be willing to engage their members in discussions around important social issues that have religious or ethical implications. Again, attenders may be engaged to assist with this.

    Church leaders might be very surprised if they know how often their well-read and well-educated members sat in the pews deeply resenting being talked down to, or hearing the Bible dumbed down to infantile levels.

25. Ministers could go out to their members' workplaces, offices, laboratories or work floors and see how their members live in their day-to-day lives. With such exposure, ministers may develop better ideas of the skill sets of their members, and imagine together with

them how their gifts might intersect with the life and vision of the church.

26. Churches could provide opportunities to develop relationships within their membership body that encourage accountability. The contemporary world of work constantly raises issues of ethical, moral and political import.

   There could be opportunities for the dispersed church community to bring to the notice of the gathered community the important questions that they are dealing with for the edification of all members. Reflection on these issues by members within the gathered community may assist those who are dealing with such issues by offering the genuine prayerful and mature discernment of the gathered church.

In case you hadn't noticed as you read this list, here are two very important observations regarding all of these suggestions:

1. Nothing in this list has a financial cost to it. Some things could perhaps be improved for a small outlay, but almost everything on the list could be done with zero impact on the church budget.

2. Nothing in this list would necessarily add more than five or ten minutes to the length of the church service, if they were properly incorporated into things that the service already entails. Many of them would add no time at all – they could just replace the focus of something that is already being done.

Conclusion

The church in the West has not in general dealt as well as it could with honouring and affirming all kinds of work, both paid and unpaid. There are systemic and cultural issues in churches that need to be re-visioned and revised.

One of the great revolutions that still needs to happen in the modern church is for the church to recapture the sense that human work is a glorious calling from God to all human beings. Once churches grasp this vision, they will take work and workers seriously. This could build solidarity between faith and work that would enrich the church and honour the image of God in humankind.

The word 'solidarity' is chosen carefully. I lived my young years in the shadow of the Cold War. No-one in the 1950s or 1960s could imagine that the great nation, the USSR, which had abandoned God and elevated labour to a form of humanistic worship in the emblem of a hammer and a sickle, could ever be defeated.

And yet ...

In the turmoil of the early years of the Second World War, a young man grew up in a Christian family in the poor suburbs of Kraków, Poland. To avoid being sent to labour camps in Germany, young Karol Wojtyla went to work in a stone quarry, serving long hours in back-breaking work with pickaxe and sledgehammer. At night he attended a clandestine, illegal seminary to train as a priest.

Years later, as Pope John Paul II, this worker–scholar–Christian, the author of the great encyclical *Laborem Exercens*, would stand up against the might of the USSR, in the Lenin Shipyard in Gdansk, celebrating Mass, and engaging the support of the workers' trade union named *Solidarność* (Solidarity). Without the workers or their Pope firing a single bullet, the USSR dissolved within a decade.

In his memoirs, Pope John Paul II quoted a poem he had written during those hard years at the quarry:

And a thought grows in me day after day:
the greatness of work is inside man.[11]

Later in the same poem, he described the death of a fellow-worker who had been killed in an accident at the quarry.

They took his body, and walked in a silent line.
Toil still lingered about him, a sense of wrong.[12]

'Work' had changed to 'toil'. This subtle, poetic change indicates the truth about human work that the young Wojtyla already sensed. Human work is a grand and noble enterprise. It is the vocation and mission[13] of humanity, all of whom are called and sent at the command of the High King, to live as faithful stewards of the creation that was spoken into being by that High King.

The task is often made difficult, reduced to mere toil, by the rebellion of other human beings who choose not to obey the royal commands, and even by the effect of the recalcitrance felt in the very fabric of the cosmos, symbolised by the cursed ground of Genesis.

But the royal command to work still stands, and we dare not call it cursed. It is good, as the Commander is good. Like the Commander, we will sometimes struggle, bleed and even die in service.

Jesus, the Perfect Human, Worker, and Son of the Owner who is also a Worker, is our role model. He calls us to work and worship in the whole of our lives, and will ultimately honour our work in the creation of the new heaven and new earth over which we will rule with him.

In both its gathered and dispersed life, the church can, if it

---

11 John Paul II, *Gift and Mystery: On the Fiftieth Anniversary of My Priestly Ordination* (New York: Doubleday Dell, 1996), p. 9.

12 Ibid., p. 10.

13 Latin: *vocare*: to call, to summon; *mitto (missum)*: to send, to dispatch.

is willing, create a *solidarity* between worker and worshipping community. That solidarity, that incarnation, will reflect the work of the Perfect Human, Jesus Christ, as he lived and worked among us, and as he graciously continues to do so, accepting our whole selves in our work as our worship.

APPENDIX

Calendar for Church Celebration of Workers and Work

This Calendar for Church Celebration of Workers and Work is intended as a model that churches could adapt to suit their own particular congregation and setting.

The Bible references are offered as suggestive guides only. They may provide a place to seek inspiration for appropriate sermons or reflections or prayers. They are *not* intended as, *nor should they be used* as 'proof texts'. Churches that follow lectionary readings may still follow the week's readings with appropriate comments and inferences.

Any idea that the Bible – an ancient book – provides direct advice on modern science or technologies in particular should be avoided. All workers should be encouraged in their doing of good work to serve a good God, through stewarding God's creation.

Calendar for church celebration of workers and work

First Sunday of month (change this to avoid special days or seasons)	Work description (to be read in as broad a sense as desired – some congregation members may be included more than once – and the list may need to be expanded)	Possible Bible references to use for preaching (Titus 3:14 and 1 Tim 3 contain basic principles)
January	All those involved in journalism, television, film, writing, music, or any of the performing arts...	Revelation 1—3 Philippians 2 Ecclesiastes Galatians 5:1–21

February	All those involved in any kind of education: students, teachers, administration assistants ...	Deuteronomy 6 Colossians 1 Proverbs 1–4 Ecclesiastes 12
March	All those involved in manual trades: carpenters, hairdressers, builders, electricians, motor mechanics ...	Exodus 31:1–11 Nehemiah 1—6 Acts 19:23ff Proverbs 10–24
April	All those involved in health arenas: doctors, medical researchers, pharmaceutics, nurses, paramedics, occupational therapists, physiotherapists, complementary medicine practitioners (chiropractors, etc.) hospital and medical centre administration and assistant staff ...	Jesus' miracles Exodus 15:22–27 Leviticus 13—15 Psalm 139:13–18
May	All those involved in government, the legal profession, public administration and civil protection: lawyers, paralegals, public servants, those in the armed services, police force and other emergency services ...	Leviticus 19–20 Exodus 20—23 Deuteronomy 16:18–20 Romans 13 Zechariah 7:8–14 Psalm 127
June	All those involved in business or commerce: business owners, banking and financial sector workers, shopkeepers, salespeople, accountants, those who work in real estate, marketing, promotions, sales ...	Micah 6:8 Romans 12 Amos 2:6–8 Leviticus 19:35–7 Acts 16:11–15

July	All those involved in science, applied science (e.g. mining and manufacturing, industrial research, design and development), information technologies, communications and allied industries …	Colossians 2 Psalms 93—99
August	All those involved in maintenance, repairs, cleaning, pest management, landscaping, manual labour of all kinds …	Leviticus 14:33–57 Proverbs 10—24
September	All those involved in volunteer or not-for-profit work, personal caring and domestic housework; stay-at-home partners, unemployed people, pensioners, retired persons …	Ruth 1 Letters of John
October	All those involved in counselling, psychology, psychiatry, mental health services, pastoral work, social services, local church paid ministry …	Esther 1—4 Jesus' healing and compassionate works 2 Corinthians 4–5 Psalms 61—64
November	All those involved in agricultural industries, marine farming, food storage, food preparation and service, tourism, hospitality …	Deuteronomy 26:5–10 Psalms 15, 33, 90, 121 1 Corinthians 12:12–31
December	All those involved in management, general administration, human resources, recruiting, occupational health and safety, compliance work, and any other worker whose field has not been covered during the year …	Proverbs 31 Nehemiah 13 Numbers 12—20 Luke 1:1–4 Philemon

REFERENCES

"Australia's Freelance Economy Grows to 4.1 Million Workers, Study Finds." *The Indian Telegraph* 27 October (2015). http://theindiantelegraph.com.au/australias-freelance-economy-grows-to-4-1-million-workers-study-finds/

Barna, George. *Revolution*. Carol Stream, IL: Tyndale House, 2005.

Barnes, Kenneth J. A. "A Theology of Work for a Post-Industrial Workplace." http://marketplaceinstitute.org/2013/02/papers-httpmarketplaceinstitute-files-wordpress-com201302a-theology-of-work-for-a-post-industrial-workplace-pdf/.

Bellamy, John, Alan Black, Keith Castle, Philip Hughes, and Peter Kaldor. *Why People Don't Go to Church*. Adelaide, SA: Openbook Publishers, 2002.

Bilton, Mark. *Monday Matters: Finding God in Your Workplace*. Mona Vale, NSW: Ark House, 2012.

Birch, Cyril, ed. *Anthology of Chinese Literature*. Vol. I. Harmondsworth, Middlesex, UK: Penguin, 1965.

Bjoraker, William D. "Word Study: (Avodah) - Work/Worship." (2016). http://ag.org/top/church_workers/wrshp_gen_avodah.cfm.

Bloom, Jon. "Jesus Came to Reverse the Curse." http://www.desiringgod.org/articles/jesus-came-to-reverse-the-curse

Bontrager, Krista. "Inspiring the Next Generation of Scientists." 12 February (2015). http://www.reasons.org/articles/Inspiring-the-Next-Generation-of-Scientists.

Bottomley, John. *Hard Work Never Killed Anybody: How the Idolisation of Work Sustains This Deadly Lie*. Northcote, VIC: Morning Star Publishing, 2015.

Brueggemann, Walter. *Genesis: Interpretation, a Biblical Commentary for Teaching and Preaching.* Atlanta, GA: John Knox, 1982.

―――. *Hopeful Imagination: Prophetic Voices in Exile.* Philadelphia, PA: Fortress Press, 1986.

Buechner, Frederick. *Wishful Thinking: A Theological Abc.* New York: Harper & Row, 1973.

Cameron, Stuart. *Faith@Work: Thistles and Thorns.* Podcast audio. Sermon preached at Newlife Uniting Church, Gold Coast 20 July, 2014. http://subsplash.com/newlifeuniting/v/b1523c3.

Camille, Alice. "Hope for Monday Mornings ". *U.S. Catholic* 80, no. 2 (Feb.1, 2015): 44-46.

Cattaneo, Peter. "The Full Monty." UK: Fox Searchlight, 1997.

"Changes in Employment and Implications for Churches (2011)." NCLS Research, 2015, http://www.ncls.org.au/default.aspx?sitemapid=138.

Chester, Tim. *Gospel-Centred Work: Becoming the Worker God Wants You to Be.* Epsom, Surrey, UK: The Good Book Company, 2013.

"Christians at Work: Examining the Intersection of Calling and Career." edited by Roxanne Stone. Ventura, CA: Barna Group, 2018.

Combs, Eugene. "Has Yhwh Cursed the Ground? Perplexity of Interpretation in Genesis 1-5." In *Ascribe to the Lord: Biblical and Other Studies in Memory of Peter C. Craigie*, edited by Lyle Eslinger and Glen Taylor. Sheffield, UK: JSOT Press, 1988.

"Connecting Liturgy with Life – an Extract." The London Institute for Contemporary Christianity, http://www.licc.org.uk/resources/connecting-liturgy-with-life-an-extract/.

Conrad, Joseph. *Heart of Darkness.* Claremont CA: Coyote Canyon Press, 2007.

Cosden, Darrell. *The Heavenly Good of Earthly Work.* Peabody, MA: Hendrickson, 2006.

Costa, Ken. *God at Work*. London: Continuum, 2007.

de Botton, Alain. *The Pleasures and Sorrows of Work*. London: Penguin, 2010.

Dodds, Canon Dr Graham. "Finding Rest." Sermon preached at Wells Cathedral, Evensong 12 October, 2014.

Dumbrell, William J. *The Search for Order: Biblical Eschatology in Focus*. Eugene, OR: Wipf and Stock, 2001.

Enns, Peter. *The Evolution of Adam: What the Bible Does and Doesn't Say About Human Origins*. Grand Rapids, MI: Brazos Press, 2012.

Foster, Richard J. *Streams of Living Water*. Bath, UK: Eagle Publishing, 1999.

Fraser, M. D., and I. J. Gordon. "Organic Matter Intake, Diet Digestibility and Feeding Behaviour of Goats, Red Deer, and South American Camelids Feeding on Three Contrasting Scottish Vegetation Communities.". *Journal of Applied Ecology* 34 (1997): 687-98.

Friesen, Garry. *Decision Making and the Will of God: A Biblical Alternative to the Traditional View*. Multnomah Publishers: Portland, OR, 1981.

Gomez, Jose H. "All You Who Labor: Towards a Spirituality of Work for the 21st Century." (2006). http://scholarship.law.nd.edu/ndjlepp/vol20/iss2/11.

Greenstone, Jody, and Matt Miller. "The Rise of the Supertemp." *Harvard Business Review* May (2012). https://hbr.org/2012/05/the-rise-of-the-supertemp.

Guinness, Os. *The Call: Finding and Fulfilling the Central Purpose of Your Life*. Nashville, TN: Word Publishing, 1998.

Haas, Martine, and Mark Mortensen. "The Secrets of Great Teamwork." *Harvard Business Review* June (2016): 71-76.

Hamilton, Victor P. *The Book of Genesis: Chapters 1-17*. Grand Rapids, MI: William B. Eerdmans, 1990.

Hammarskjold, Dag. *Markings*. Translated by Leif Sjoberg and W. H. Auden. New York: Alfred A. Knopf, 1969.

Hardy, Lee. *The Fabric of This World: Inquiries into Calling, Career Choice, and the Design of Human Work.* Grand Rapids, MI: William. B. Eerdmans, 1990.

Harrison, Peter. "Religion, the Royal Society, and the Rise of Science." *Theology and Science* 6, no. 3 (2008): 255-71.

Hart, Ian. "The Teaching of Luther and Calvin About Ordinary Work: 1. Martin Luther (1483–1546)." *Evangelical Quarterly* 67, no. 1 (1995): 35-52.

Hauerwas, Stanley. *Matthew.* Brazos Theological Commentary on the Bible. edited by R. R. Reno Grand Rapids, MI: Brazos Press, 2006.

Hazony, Yoram. *God and Politics in Esther.* New York: Cambridge University Press, 2016.

Hertz, J. H., ed. *Pentateuch and Haftorahs.* London: Soncino Press, 1960.

Heschel, Abraham Joshua. *The Prophets.* Vol. 1, New York: Harper & Row, 1969.

———. *The Sabbath.* New York: Noonday Press, 1979.

Howarth, Brad. "Future of Work: How Nab and Microsoft Are Creating Tomorrow's Workplace Today." *Business Review Weekly* 14 April (2014). http://www.brw.com. au/p/leadership/future_workplace_work_today_nab_ xd7t3IlKb0SMrBHVecFi9H.

John Paul II. *Gift and Mystery: On the Fiftieth Anniversary of My Priestly Ordination.* New York: Doubleday Dell, 1996.

———. *Laborem Exercens (on Human Work): Encyclical Letter of the Supreme Pontiff on Human Work.* Vatican, 1981. http://w2.vatican.va/content/john-paul-ii/en/encyclicals/ documents/hf_jp-ii_enc_14091981_laborem-exercens.html

Kaldor, Peter. *Who Goes Where? Who Doesn't Care?* Homebush West, NSW: Lancer, 1987.

Keller, Timothy. *Every Good Endeavor: Connecting Your Work to God's Work.* New York: Dutton, 2012.

Kelly, Geffrey B., and F. Burton Nelson, eds. *A Testament to Freedom: The Essential Writings of Dietrich Bonhoeffer*. San Francisco: Harper, 1990.

Krznaric, Roman. *How to Find Fulfilling Work*. London: Macmillan, 2012.

Lancaster, John. "Leveling the Playing Field." *Time* February 4–11 (2019): 75-77.

Langer, Richard. "Niggle's Leaf and Holland's Opus: Reflections on the Theological Significance of Work." *Evangelical Review of Theology* 33, no. 2 (2009): 100-17.

Larive, Armand. *After Sunday: A Theology of Work*. New York: Continuum, 2004.

Lawrence, Brother. *The Practice of the Presence of God*. Translated by E. M. Blaiklock. London: Hodder and Stoughton, 1981.

Leo, Graham. "Reading the Book of Esther: A Theology of Work for the 21st Century in the West." *Zadok* Summer, no. 133 (2016): 8-12.

Lewis, C. S. *God in the Dock*. Grand Rapids, MI: William B. Eerdmans, 1970.

———. *Mere Christianity*. New York: Macmillan, 1952.

"Litany for the Workplace." Centre for Faith and Work, http:// www.centerforfaithandwork.com/node/789?utm_ source=MMM+1st+January+2015&utm_ campaign=MMM+1-8-15&utm_medium=email.

Mackenzie, Alistair. "The Future for 'Faith at Work': A New Zealand Perspective." In *The Diaconal Church: Beyond the Mould of Christendom*, edited by David Clark. Peterborough, England: Fastprint Publishing, 2017.

Marshall, Colin, and Tony Payne. *The Trellis and the Vine*. Kingsford, NSW: Matthias Media, 2009.

Mason, Paul. *Postcapitalism: A Guide to Our Future*. London: Penguin, 2016.

Mathews, Kenneth A. *Genesis 1–11:26, Vol.1a*. The New American Commentary. Nashville, TN: Broadman & Holman, 2002.

McGrath, Alister. *The Future of Christianity*. Oxford: Blackwell Publishers, 2002.

Messenger, Will. "Gifts That Differ; Callings That Unite. An Interview with Will Messenger." *Christian History Institute*, no. 110 (2014): 4-6.

Middleton, J. Richard. *The Liberating Image: The Imago Dei in Genesis 1*. Grand Rapids, MI: Brazos, 2005.

"Midrash Tanhuma." http://www.sacred-texts.com/jud/midrash.htm.

Miller, David W. *God at Work: The History and Promise of the Faith at Work Movement*. New York: Oxford University Press, 2007.

Miller, Keith B. "Theological Implications of an Evolving Creation." *Perspectives on Science and Christian Faith* 45, no. 3 (1993): 150-60.

Moltmann, Jurgen. *On Human Dignity: Political Theology and Ethics*. Philadelphia, PA: Fortress Press, 1984.

Monjardino, Miguel. "A Liberal Education." *City Journal* Autumn (2013): 1.

Niditch, Susan. *Chaos to Cosmos: Studies in Biblical Patterns of Creation*. Chico, CA: Scholars Press, 1985.

Oakeshott, Michael. "Work and Play." *First Things* June/July(1995). http://www.firstthings.com/article/2008/09/003-work-and-play-15

Ostring, Elizabeth. "The Theology of Human Work as Found in the Genesis Narrative Compared with the Co-Creationist Theology of Human Work." Ph. D. Thesis submitted to The Faculty of Theology, Avondale College of Higher Education, NSW: http://research.avondale.edu.au/cgi/viewcontent.cgi?article=1003&context=theses_phd, 2015.

Oxford Dictionaries. Oxford University, 2016. http://www.oxforddictionaries.com/definition/english/viceroy.

Patterson, Roger. "Labor: A Blessing and a Curse." https://answersingenesis.org/sin/labor-blessing-curse/

Peel, Bill. "Does Your Work Matter in God's Eyes?" Centre for Faith and Work, LeTourneau University, http://www.centerforfaithandwork.com/node/729?utm_source=MMM+1st+August+Send+8/10/15&utm_campaign=MMM+1st+Aug+email+8/10/15&utm_medium=email cited 8 Feb., 2016.

Pinnock, Clark H. "Climbing out of the Swamp: The Evangelical Struggle to Understand the Creation Texts." *Interpretation* XLIII, no. 2 (1989): 143-55.

Pittman, Frank. *Man Enough: Fathers, Sons, and the Search for Masculinity*. New York: Perigee Press, 1993.

Preece, Gordon R. *The Viability of the Vocation Tradition in Trinitarian, Credal and Reformed Perspective: The Threefold Call*. New York: The Edwin Mellen Press, 1998.

Radner, Ephraim. *Hope among the Fragments: The Broken Church and Its Engagement of Scripture*. Grand Rapids, MI: Brazos Press, 2004.

Russell, Mark L. "The Secret of Marketplace Leadership Success: Constructing a Comprehensive Framework for the Effective Integration of Leadership, Faith, and Work." *Journal of Religious Leadership* 6, no. 1 (2007).

Ryken, Leland. *Work and Leisure in Christian Perspective*. Eugene, OR: Wipf and Stock Publishers, 1987.

Sacks, Jonathan. *To Heal a Fractured World: The Ethics of Responsibility*. London: Continuum, 2005.

Sayers, Dorothy. *Letters to a Diminished Church*. New York: W Publishing Group, 2004.

Schiller, Ben. "Welcome to the Post-Work Economy." 15 March(2016). http://www.fastcoexist.com/3056483/welcome-to-the-post-work-economy.

Smith, James K. A. "Naturalizing "Shalom": Confessions of a Kuyperian Secularist." *Cardus* (June 28, 2013). https://www.cardus.ca/comment/article/3993/naturalizing-shalom-confessions-of-a-kuyperian-secularist/.

Snyder, Howard. *Global Good News*. Nashville, TN: Abingdon Press, 2001.

Sorkin, Aaron, John Wells, Thomas Schlamme, Llewellyn Wells, Eli Attie, Debora Cahn, and et al. W. G. Walden. "The West Wing the Complete Series." Directed by Michael Lehmann, Warner Home Video, 2006.

Srnicek, Nick, and Alex Williams. *Inventing the Future: Postcapitalism and a World without Work*. London: Verso Books, 2015.

"State of Work in Australia." Reventure, in association with Barna, 2016.

Steenberg, M. C. *Irenaeus on Creation: The Cosmic Christ and the Saga of Redemption*. Leiden, Netherlands: Brill, 2008.

Stevens, R. Paul. *The Abolition of the Laity: Vocation, Work, and Ministry in Biblical Perspective*. Carlisle, UK: Paternoster, 1999.

The McCrindle Blog. "Church Attendance in Australia (Infographic) 2013." McCrindle, http://www.mccrindle.com.au/the-mccrindle-blog/church_attendance_in_australia_infographic.

Tolkien, Christopher, ed. *J. R. R. Tolkien: The Monsters and the Critics and Other Essays*. London: HarperCollins, 1983.

Tolkien, J. R. R. "Leaf by Niggle." In *The Tolkien Reader*, 100-20. New York: Ballantine, 1978.

———. *The Lord of the Rings*. London: HarperCollins, 2002.

"TV Tropes." http://tvtropes.org/pmwiki/pmwiki.php/Main/UnconfessedUnemployment cited January, 2016.

Veith, Gene Edward, Jr. *God at Work: Your Christian Vocation in All of Life*. Wheaton, IL: Crossway, 2002.

Venema, Dennis R., and Scot McKnight. *Adam and the Genome: Reading Scripture after Genetic Science*. Grand Rapids, MI.: BrazosPress, 2017.

Volf, Miroslav. *Work in the Spirit: Toward a Theology of Work*. Eugene, OR: Wipf and Stock Publishers, 2001.

von Rad, Gerhard. *Genesis: A Commentary (Revised Edition)*. Philadelphia, PA: The Westminster Press, 1972.

Wald, Jeff. "Five Predictions for the Freelance Economy in 2016." *Forbes* 9 December (2015). http://www.forbes.com/sites/waldleventhal/2015/12/09/5-predictions-for-the-freelance-economy-in-2016/#357c631d63d7.

Walton, John H. *The Lost World of Adam and Eve: Genesis 2–3 and the Human Origins Debate*. Downers Grove, IL: IVP Academic, 2015.

Westermann, Claus. *Creation*. Translated by John J. Scullion. London: SPCK, 1974.

———. *Genesis 1–11: A Commentary*. Translated by John J. Scullion. London: SPCK, 1984.

Whelchel, Hugh. *How Then Should We Work? Rediscovering the Biblical Doctrine of Work*. Bloomington, IN: WestBow Press, 2012.

White, Louis. "Why Aren't Gen Y Satisfied?" *Sydney Morning Herald*, 17 May, 2016.

Wiki, Tolkien Gateway. "Eucatastrophe." http://tolkiengateway.net/wiki/Eucatastrophe.

Wingren, Gustaf. *Luther on Vocation*. Translated by Carl C. Rasmussen. Eugene, OR: Wipf & Stock, 2004.

Witherington, Ben, III. *Work: A Kingdom Perspective on Labor*. Grand Rapids, MI: William B. Eerdmans, 2011.

Wright, Christopher J. H. *Old Testament Ethics for the People of God*. Downers Grove, IL: InterVarsity Press, 2004.

Wright, N. T. *Virtue Reborn*. London: SPCK, 2010.

Wright, Tom. *The Day the Revolution Began*. London: SPCK, 2016.

Yeago, David S. "The Catholic Luther." *First Things* Vol. 61, March (1996): 37-41.

Zimmerli, Walter. *Old Testament Theology in Outline*. Edinburgh: T. & T. Clark Ltd, 1978.